MASTERS OF THE ITALIAN LINE

Leonardo da Vinci

Michelangelo and *Raffaello*

Ian Sebire

AMBERLEY

First published 2018

Amberley Publishing
The Hill, Stroud, Gloucestershire, GL5 4EP
www.amberley-books.com

Copyright © Ian Sebire, 2018

The right of Ian Sebire to be identified as the
Author of this work has been asserted in accordance with
the Copyright, Designs and Patents Act 1988.

ISBN 978 1 4456 8350 8 (print)
ISBN 978 1 4456 8351 5 (ebook)

British Library Cataloguing in Publication Data.
A catalogue record for this book is available from the
British Library.

Origination by Amberley Publishing.
Printed in Great Britain.

Introduction

Counter-intuitively, the advent of jet airliners in the late 1950s prompted a flurry of activity in the shipyards of Europe. Nowhere was output more prolific than Italy, which was still recovering from the trauma of being torn apart, physically and politically, by the Second World War. Despite inherent instability, this period witnessed an economic miracle, during which the country outperformed all other European nations. Italian products became sought after worldwide and its technical and engineering expertise, particularly in the northern industrial heartlands, defied the post-war Continental gloom. Buoyed by this renewed confidence and significant government investment, shipbuilding and shipping flourished.

Some of this new tonnage enjoyed long and successful careers. Generally they were the privately owned vessels, whose adaptable design and management facilitated a smooth transition when waning liner service transformed into the expanding cruise trade. In contrast, the state-owned ships were often pure-bred liners, built expressly to convey a spectrum of social classes from one continent to another as quickly as possible. Myopic management, shielded from commercial reality by generous state subsidies, often lacked either the will or means to adapt.

The Italian Line's last three new-builds fall into the latter category. Although *Leonardo da Vinci* enjoyed early profitability and enduring popularity, *Michelangelo* and *Raffaello*, with their protracted gestation and design deficiencies, never really stood a chance. Ridiculed as the 'make work' ships, ten years in service was scant return on their $160 million price tag.

Nevertheless, to analyse their careers by such narrow criteria misses the point. *Leonardo da Vinci*, *Michelangelo* and *Raffaello* were among the last examples of 'Ships of State' – flag bearers built in domestic yards, designed, owned and crewed by their fellow countrymen, with (initially at least) the blessing and financial assistance of government. They were Italian ambassadors, peripatetic galleries of contemporary art and a microcosm of the nation that helped to illuminate the twilight era of the ocean liner. Furthermore, they enriched the lives of those fortunate souls who sailed and worked on them, as well as the many more who watched admiringly from the shore and even those, like myself, who have simply read about their exploits, probably through rose-tinted spectacles.

I hope that this book will add something to their story, honouring these magnificent vessels and the crews that sailed them.

Above left: Masters of the Italian Line, *Leonardo da Vinci*, *Michelangelo* and *Raffaello*, in a painting by the author. (www.sarniawatercolours.co.uk)

Above right: The only occasion all three ships were in port together; 31 January 1969. (Giancarlo Criscuolo collection)

CHAPTER 1

Leonardo da Vinci: The Unique Flagship

Alberto Imparato's beautiful acrylic painting of *Leonardo da Vinci* at sea, sporting her original black hull. (Alberto Imparato)

That an object of such exceptional beauty should be borne out of tragedy seems inconceivable. Yet the story of *Leonardo da Vinci* starts on the sultry evening of 25 July 1956, in the fog-shrouded approaches to New York. That night, a combination of inclement weather and human fallibility resulted in the ice-strengthened bow of the Swedish cargo liner *Stockholm* mortally puncturing the starboard flank of the Italian Line's *Andrea Doria*. The Italian flagship sank early the following day. Just one day later the company board met and approved plans for a replacement. By the end of the month the Italian Government had authorised a 50 billion lire loan towards construction costs, and on 8 August 1956, less than two weeks after *Andrea Doria* capsized off the Nantucket coast, a provisional agreement was signed with Cantiere Navale Ansaldo at Sestri Ponente (Ansaldo).

In hindsight, the swiftness of Italy's actions can appear insensitive; after all, fifty-one people lost their lives along with the national flagship. Nevertheless, such judgements ignore the pervading national spirit at the time, with politicians, public and the media vowing in unison to avenge their loss. There was also a financial incentive. The Benni Law of 1936 (named after the minister who introduced it), which provided for generous state shipbuilding subsidies, was due to expire at the end of 1956.

Above: Daybreak on 26 July 1956. Mobbed by prying aircraft, forlorn and abandoned, *Andrea Doria* awaits her fate; note the port side lifeboats impotently still in their davits. (Bill Miller collection)

Below: In contrast to her sister, *Cristoforo Colombo* enjoyed longevity as the Italian Line's most popular and versatile post-war liner. After *Andrea Doria*'s untimely demise she assumed the mantle of flagship until joined by *Leonardo da Vinci* on the *linea espresso* from 1960 to 1965. When the superliners arrived she took over from the *Vulcania* and *Saturnia*, boosting trade on the Adriatic service to New York, before ultimately transferring to the La Plata route, also from Trieste, until March 1977. After a stint as an accommodation ship for construction workers in Venezuela, she finally succumbed to the cutters torch at Kaohsiung, Taiwan, in 1983. (Bill Miller collection)

The design of the new ship reappraised blueprints of the *Andrea Doria* and *Cristoforo Colombo* twins, incorporating several safety modifications in light of the former's sinking. Fourteen watertight bulkheads were installed, with thirteen of these extending from the double bottom right to Upper Deck. Equally significant was the firefighting equipment, including a comprehensive sprinkler system.

The twelve lifeboats were held on Welin 'pure-pivot' davits, eschewing conventional gravity davits and allowing the boats to be safely launched even with a 25 degree list. (Ansaldo, Italia – Alberto Imparato collection)

Perhaps the most controversial modification was the decision to incorporate two entirely separate and autonomous engine rooms, allowing the ship to maintain power and propulsion even if one room was holed or disabled. Doubtless well intentioned and an engineering *tour de force*, it meant the ship needed all boilers online for efficient sailing, resulting in proportionally higher fuel costs. Here one of *Leonardo da Vinci*'s turbines is hoisted aboard. (Ansaldo, Italia – Alberto Imparato collection)

In addition, the new vessel also included elements of planned 36,000 grt replacements for the *Vulcania* and *Saturnia*. Allocated yard No. 1550, on 23 June 1957 the keel was laid on the same slip as her ill-fated predecessor. The previous week the Italian Line had revealed she would be named *Leonardo da Vinci* in honour of the great artist and inventor. Being the offspring of fate, *Leonardo da Vinci* was unique among Italy's post-war new-builds as the only vessel without a sister.

Inevitably, the spectre of *Andrea Doria* cast a shadow over the new vessel. Conscious of this, the Italian Line launched a concerted publicity campaign to promote the artistic and technological qualities of their new liner, characteristics that her namesake would have been proud of. Central to this promotion was a 7.5-metre-long model of the ship, introduced at the Paris International Exhibition of 1958 and subsequently displayed on a tour of European and North American cities. Among a plethora of facts and figures was the company's assertion that *Leonardo da Vinci*'s machinery spaces had been designed to allow easy conversion to a nuclear power plant 'at some future time in the 1960s'.

Initial proposals that she would be in service by the end of 1959 proved over optimistic. Nevertheless, the Italian Line was impatient to have its new flagship in service. Since the demise of *Andrea Doria*,

A magazine advert for the new ship, dominated by her namesake's self-portrait in old age. Nino Zoncado's functional First Class foyer included a silver high-relief impression of the portrait by Marino Renato Mazzacurati. The diminutive ship's profile includes screening forward of the funnel, which appears to have been an early design feature that was subsequently dropped. (Author's collection)

TRIBUTE
TO GENIUS

THE LEONARDO DA VINCI On July 9th Italian Line's new flagship, the incomparable Leonardo da Vinci, will sail into New York. Italian Line is proud to name its new masterpiece after a creator of masterpieces. As Leonardo summed up the arts and sciences of his era, so his namesake expresses the total genius of modern Italian art and engineering. A few statistics: 761 feet of elegance (about 3 city blocks); 33,500 splendid tons; 11 decks; 5 tiled swimming pools (2 for children); accommodations for 1,300 pleasure-loving passengers. Maiden voyage to the Mediterranean: July 16th. Look for a trans-ocean masterpiece—on July 9th. *Italian Line*

Battery Park Building, 24 State Street, New York 4, N.Y. • Telephone: Digby 4-0800

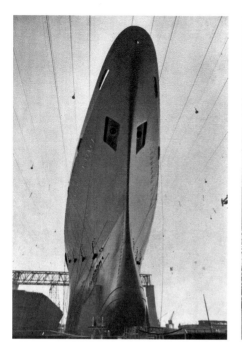

Above left: The beautifully sculpted 765.8-foot-long hull that emerged on the Ansaldo slipway featured a sharp, heavily raked bow, in marked contrast to the 'knuckle' on *Cristoforo Colombo*. Her 91.1-foot beam was devoid of the tumblehome that characterised the earlier liners, leading to a smoothly rounded stern. (Ansaldo, Italia – Alberto Imparato collection)

Above right: There was a jubilant atmosphere throughout Genoa and its environs on 7 December 1958 as a vast crowd of 80,000 gathered at Sestri Ponente. Signora Carla Gronchi, wife of the Italian President, named the vibrant red hull, resplendent in its primer undercoat. Urged on by the cheering hordes, *Leonardo da Vinci* glided down the ways and entered her element for the first time. (Ansaldo, Italia – Alberto Imparato collection)

makeshift plans had seen *Giulio Cesare* and *Augustus* switch from their regular South American service to the express New York route, while *Conte Grande* and *Conte Biancamano* also made cameo appearances.

In April 1960, *Leonardo da Vinci* was ready for trials. Externally there was a clear family relationship to *Cristoforo Colombo*, with the general arrangement in keeping with all previous post-war Italian new-builds, a single mast atop the wheelhouse and a large, centrally placed funnel. This conventional profile was lauded by traditionalists in marked contrast to contempories *Canberra*, *Oriana* and *Rotterdam*. The stack was taller and longer than *Cristoforo Colombo*'s, featuring a conventional grill at the top and a small projecting soot shield. Its additional length and position 50 feet aft of centre was required to accommodate the uptakes from the two distinct machinery spaces. *Leonardo da Vinci* had a more angular superstructure arrangement, a feature accentuated by an additional deck (ten passenger decks in total) compared to her predecessors.

The forward holds provided 91,076 cubic feet of cargo space and there was garaging for up to sixty cars. The access hatch was serviced by booms attached to two kingposts on the foredeck.

The layout of public rooms and accommodation was dictated by the Line's adherence to a three-class structure. In marked contrast to the egalitarian horizontal subdivision adopted by contemporaries *Rotterdam* and *France*, *Leonardo da Vinci*'s vertical delineation was little changed from ships of the Edwardian era. This created a disjointed passenger flow with First Class located centrally and on upper

Right: Shipyard workers prepare Belvedere Deck for its teak planking. The photograph appears to date from December 1959; a Christmas tree is perched on top of the mast. (Ansaldo, Italia – Alberto Imparato collection)

Below: Cargo capacity was significantly reduced, and was in fact eliminated entirely from the stern, which now provided swimming pools and lido space for each of the three classes with an overall outdoor deck space amounting to 32,000 square feet. Devoid of cranes and the associated hatches, the tiered aft decks descended in an elegantly stepped arrangement. The First Class lido was the largest such space on any liner at the time and was infrared-heated for year-round use. This publicity material view was taken after *Leonardo da Vinci* was repainted with a white hull in February 1966. (Author's collection)

The Living Is Easy... *Cruise Life is carefree on the palatial resort afloat called Leonardo da Vinci*

Between your visits to fascinating ports, an unforgettable vacation awaits you on the ship known for its wealth of resort pleasures . . . your luxurious hotel throughout the cruise. Designed especially for the outdoor living that the milder climate of the Sunny Southern Route calls for, the great LEONARDO offers you several outdoor swimming pools and acres of spacious decks to play and relax on . . . exciting, congenial activities in a host of beautiful public rooms, dancing, partying, entertainment, movies, masquerades . . . gastronomic triumphs created by famed master chefs as well as special diets for individual requirements. And at all times, the Italian Line reputation for impeccable service is shown to advantage.

33,500 gross tons. Length overall 761 ft. Beam 91 ft. Completely air conditioned with individual controls. Ten decks. Cruising speed 23 knots. 5 outdoor pools (3 for adults, 2 for children). 30 public rooms. Closed-circuit television in public rooms, suites and de luxe cabins, 4 automatic stabilizer fins. Ship-to-shore radio telephone.

decks, Cabin Class adjacent to First Class and lower, and Tourist Class restricted to the extremities, far forward, aft and deep in the hull. This was especially illustrated on the promenade deck, which incorporated from bow to stern the cinema/theatre (open to all), First Class ballroom, lounge and bar, the Cabin Class ballroom/lounge and cocktail bar, and then, farthest aft, the Tourist Class lido, swimming pool and veranda bar. The encircling enclosed promenade was similarly broken up. Tourist Class passengers in particular were kept fit transiting between their respective segments.

An invitation only competition was held to decide on the appointment of interior designers for the new flagship, with a panel of judges including Italian Line executives chaired by art historian Giulio Carlo Argan. The selection of veteran Gustavo Pulitzer-Finali as co-ordinating architect with prominent roles for the experienced Matteo Langoni and Nino Zoncado indicated a conservative approach. However, Argan strongly advocated the work of shipboard debutants Vincenza Monaco and Amedeo Luccichenti, whose reputations had been forged designing modernist buildings in Rome. They produced the sequence of First and Cabin Class public rooms on the promenade deck, which became a significant element of the ship's success and popularity.

A colour photograph of the First Class ballroom, known as the Arras Room. The photograph shows the structural symmetry, earthy toned upholstery and oatmeal-coloured carpet, which perfectly matched the mahogany ribbing of the ceiling and walls. (Ansaldo, Italia – Alberto Imparato collection)

The First Class central lounge and adjacent bar, also by Monaco and Luccichenti, continued the nautical theme set by the Arras Room. (Ansaldo, Italia – Alberto Imparato collection)

Above left: Nino Zoncado's First Class dining room was adorned with bronze sculptures by Marcello Mascherini. (Ansaldo, Italia – Alberto Imparato collection)

Above right: An Italian Line publicity image of the First Class children's room on *Leonardo da Vinci*, normally filled with noisy little ones. (Author's collection)

Below: A spacious First Class cabin on *Leonardo da Vinci*. (Ansaldo, Italia – Don Leavitt collection)

Above left: The beautiful Cabin Class lounge/ballroom by Monaco and Luccichenti was called the Paintings Room after the spectrum of contemporary art displayed within it. (Ansaldo, Italia – Alberto Imparato collection)

Above right: A brightly decorated Cabin Class cabin. (Ansaldo, Italia – Alberto Imparato collection)

Below: *Leonardo da Vinci's* Tourist Class social room with a dance floor populated by sedentary couples in this Italian Line publicity photograph. (Author's collection)

Above: *Leonardo da Vinci*'s Tourist Class dining room. (Author's collection)

Right: Although 75 per cent of Tourist Class cabins had en-suite facilities, most were small and located far aft and forward on the lower decks of the *Leonardo da Vinci*. (Author's collection)

Above: A company first, the 225-seat theatre/cinema was forward on the promenade deck and was arranged athwartship (sideways) to maximise space. (Ansaldo, Italia – Alberto Imparato collection)

Below: The ship's chapel, a haven for quiet contemplation and the scene of regular Mass. In a tragic twist of irony, the chapel was also the source of the ultimate inferno that consumed the ship. (Italian Line – Author's collection)

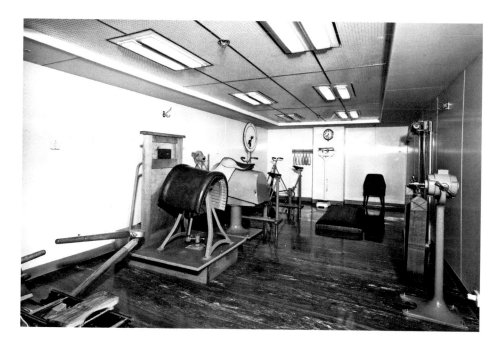

Above: The gym on board *Leonardo da Vinci* included the most modern equipment of the time, which appears nostalgically quaint by today's standards. (Ansaldo, Italia – Alberto Imparato collection)

Below: A stylised *Leonardo da Vinci* brochure cover. (Don Leavitt collection)

LEONARDO DA VINCI

Italian Line

Pier-side 'basin' trials were undertaken in April, revealing an immediate flaw. The serene exterior belied a fundamental stability problem, ostensibly caused by the additional superstructure deck. To compensate and lower the ship's centre of gravity, 500 tons of permanent cement ballast was installed in the bowels of the ship. This resolved the dangerous 'top hammer' and helped the ship develop a cherished reputation as a good sea boat (also helped by the pair of Denny Brown stabilisers – a company first), but at a cost. The additional tonnage increased the draft to 31 feet and as a consequence upped the fuel required to maintain her service speed. So as well as enhancing her stability she earned another, less favourable reputation, for her voracious appetite for Bunker C oil.

Following engine trials the previous day, *Leonardo da Vinci* was manoeuvred into the dry dock at Genoa on 10 May 1960 to have her underwater hull prepared for sea trials. Three days later the new vessel edged out of her home port, perfectly reflected in the still, glassy waters of the Gulf of Genoa, for endurance trials. She maintained her contract speed of 23 knots for a full 36 hours and in the course of acceptance trials on the 19 May 1960 achieved a top speed of 25.6 knots, sustaining an impressive 25.41 knot average for 9 hours. The Italian Line President, Giuseppe Zuccoli, proudly accepted the new national flagship in the handing over ceremony on 15 June 1960. On 18 June Genoa's Archbishop Siri consecrated the ship's chapel and the bell was installed, a poignant gift from the town of Vinci, her namesakes birthplace. Later the same day she sailed on a shakedown cruise, calling at the island of Caprera, off Sardinia's north-eastern coast (where dignitaries laid a wreath at the tomb of Giuseppe Garibaldi, in honour of his role in the unification of Italy a century before), followed by Barcelona and Cannes.

A week later, on a beautiful mid-summer's day, *Leonardo da Vinci* steamed out of Genoa on her maiden voyage. As 1,222 passengers settled into their unfamiliar surroundings, rumours circulated that among their number were *Andrea Doria* survivors, and initially at least her predecessor was on the collective mind. After calling at Cannes, Naples and Gibraltar, she bisected the Pillars of Hercules and steamed out into the Atlantic. As the voyage progressed the shadow of *Andrea Doria* dissipated – even a storm encountered two days out failed to dampen the atmosphere, with the weather simply proving the value of the stabilisers, which eliminated the majority of rolling.

Nine days after she left her homeland, Italy's new flagship arrived in New York for the first time, receiving a tumultuous welcome as she berthed alongside Pier 84 at 13.00 on 9 July 1960.

The most beautiful passenger ship ever built? Certainly a contender, *Leonardo da Vinci* powers along the Liguria coast on her sea trials. (Claudio Serra collection)

Above: To a fanfare of salutes from neighbouring vessels resonating around Genoa harbour, *Leonardo da Vinci* cast off on her first transatlantic crossing. Dressed overall and accompanied by an assortment of tugs and pleasure craft, the new flagship presented a magnificent sight. (Archivio Publifoto Genova – Claudio Serra collection)

Below: With the sun streaming through the misty Manhattan skyline, *Leonardo da Vinci*, escorted by celebratory fountains from fireboats and a retinue of tugs, proudly steams up the Hudson. Any lingering melancholy over events four summers previous had been dispelled, and a festive atmosphere prevailed. (Bill Miller collection)

CHAPTER 2
Michelangelo and *Raffaello*: Glorious Follies

A Tutta Forza by Ian Sebire. (www.sarniawatercolours.co.uk)

> Folly   1. Foolishness, a foolish act, behaviour, idea etc.
>   2. A costly ornamental building that serves no practical purpose.

In commercial terms, either of these dictionary definitions could be deemed appropriate for categorising the Italian Line's last new-builds and their largest liners of the post-war era. *Michelangelo* and *Raffaello* were magnificent, fast, luxurious vessels, but were also outmoded, uneconomic anachronisms. Each was a maritime folly.

Proposals for two new vessels for the New York run originated in 1958, the same year in which airliners usurped ocean liners as the mode of choice for passengers crossing between Europe and the USA. In spite of this momentous swing away from sea travel, the Italian Line was not alone in its preoccupation with new tonnage. The French Line and Cunard also planned new giants for transatlantic service, citing the general increase in numbers making their way across 'the pond', even if the sea-going element was diminishing. Although theoretically replacements for the veteran *Vulcania* and *Saturnia*, they were always envisaged as express 'superliners' on the *linea espresso* Genoa to

New York service. Initial rumours were that the new ships would be named after the Italian scientists and inventors Enrico Fermi and Guglielmo Marconi.

Designs for the flagships were developed by teams from the two principal Italian shipbuilders, Ansaldo at Sestri Ponente near Genoa and Cantieri Riuniti dell'Adriatico (CRDA) with its facilities on Italy's Adriatic shore. It would have been interesting to see whether CRDA's design (like their contemporary *Oceanic*) could have made the transition to cruising that the actual ships so patently failed to achieve. Although conceived as a dual function transatlantic liner with off-season cruising capability, *Oceanic* entered service as a dedicated cruise ship, garnering praise and profits for her owners. Instead the Italian Line board adopted Ansaldo's design for what amounted to a larger, stretched, twin-stack version of *Leonardo da Vinci*.

Above: *Enrico Fermi* by Ian Sebire. CRDA's design proposal incorporated the radical hull design patented by its chief naval architect, Nicolo Costanzi, featuring a 'swan neck' convex/concave bow and a hybrid spoon and transom stern arrangement. A solitary, streamlined funnel and bridge-top radar mast complemented the curved forward superstructure, which also incorporated a lounge above the bridge – at the time a radical departure from convention. Had this design prevailed they would certainly have been stunning ships. (Ian Sebire)

Below: Early Italian Line publicity material included this cutaway image of *Michelangelo*. With the exception of the three-deck-high cinema aft and the First Class Lido forward of the funnels, the basic configuration mirrored that on *Leonardo da Vinci*. (Author's collection)

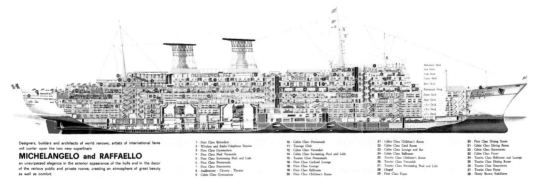

Initial images portrayed ships with a pair of conventional ovoid funnels, heightened conical versions of that found on their predecessor. Uniquely among Italian post-war new-builds, and atypical of contemporaries, the ships also featured two masts. Those first artist's impressions also showed them with the traditional black-hulled livery and white sheer line then carried by all the company's designated North Atlantic liners. Although when completed the ships would bear only a tenuous resemblance to that initial image; the changes, while visually dramatic, were essentially cosmetic. The Italian Line had steadfastly refused to change their three-class configuration, which was just one of a number of design flaws that ultimately foreshortened the ships' seagoing careers.

A state of euphoria suffused the company on 4 February 1960 as the Italian Line placed firm orders for the new express liners. Although logically and logistically it would have made sense to award the contract to a single yard, the political imperative was to share the work and thereby spread employment. Inevitably the contract for one of these new flagships was awarded to the designer Ansaldo at Genoa, builders of *Cristoforo Colombo, Andrea Doria* and the recently completed *Leonardo da Vinci*. For a final time (subsequent vessels were constructed in graving docks) the first keel plate of yard No. 1577 was hoisted onto the blocks of slipway No. 1 on 8 September 1960, where *Rex* had been constructed thirty years before. On that same late summer's day, at CRDA's Trieste facility, the first element of yard No. 1864 (the future *Raffaello*) was also set in place after a blessing from the city's bishop. Simultaneously, along the coast at Monfalcone, the keels of Lloyd Triestino's new sister ships (also part of the state-owned FINMARE shipping group) for their Australia service were laid down. While co-ordinating these ceremonies certainly garnered a good deal of publicity, ultimately building these four large liners in the same country at the same time was too great a logistical challenge. Delays were endemic. A shortage of steel and skilled labour, compounded by strikes, slowed construction dramatically. Originally the keel laying was due to coincide with *Leonardo da Vinci*'s maiden voyage in June 1960; the first of many deadlines had been missed.

Towering majestically above the ceremonial platform and in front of an enthusiastic gathering of 100,000 spectators, the first of the twins was named *Michelangelo* by Donna Laura Segni, wife of the Italian President, on 16 September 1962. Overhead, jets of the Italian Air Force circled in tribute as the hull was taken in tow to the adjacent fitting out berth.

ᴛᴠMICHELANGELO
ᴛᴠRAFFAELLO

THE LARGEST, FASTEST AND MOST MODERN LINERS IN SERVICE BETWEEN NORTH AMERICA AND THE MEDITERRANEAN

(beginning in 1965)

● Gross tonnage 43,000	● New concept in funnel construction to assure the deflection of smoke and soot from the immediate area of the ship.
● Maximum speed . . . . 29 knots	
● Cruising speed . . . . 26.5 knots	● Fire-proof and sound-proof material used throughout.
● Length . . . . 905 feet	● Twin stabilizers with 4 retractable fins to reduce rolling under the severest conditions.
● Beam . . . . 102 feet	● Two radar systems.
● Height to the top deck . . . . 113 feet	● Air conditioning with individual controls in every cabin to assure greatest comfort in every season.

Italy ←— 7 days —→ New York ←— 5 days —→ Gibraltar

Early artist impression of the new ships with their projected vital statistics. (Author's collection)

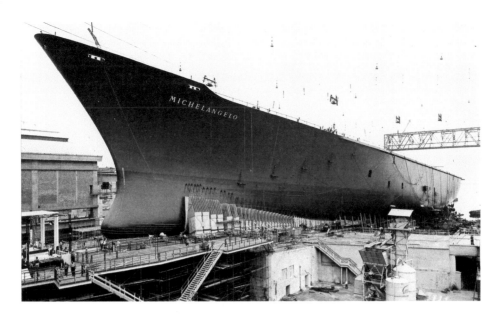

Above: It took two years to complete the hulls. At 902 feet they were the longest Italian liners of all, with a shape that was a synthesis of horizontal stern and amidships with a dramatically rising, flared bow. A svelte block co-efficient of 0.565 was the finest of any Italian liner; from the bulbous forefoot to the rounded spoon stern, the hull was of an all-welded construction. (Archivo Publifoto Genoa – Claudio Serra collection)

Below: The crowd's collective cheers mingle with the tortuous groans and screams of hull and cradle chaffing on the heavily greased slipway. As the stern reaches the water's edge, propellers claw at the sea and the hull pivots as the buoyant aft section rises. She creates a wave that swamps surrounding jetties and causes the numerous small spectator boats to buck in unison. However, all is controlled and she will soon be tethered by the 550 tons of drag chains, which will be released in sequence with deafening precision. (Archivo Publifoto Genoa – Claudio Serra collection)

At Trieste there were even greater delays. A full six months after *Michelangelo*, under a clear, cobalt sky, *Raffaello* was launched into the Adriatic on 24 March 1963, after being named by Donna Giuliana Merzagora, wife of the President of the Italian Senate. In fact, with promenade deck completed, she was only three months behind her sister's schedule.

Slowly over the ensuing year, both ships started to take shape. Although the angular superstructures showed a clear family resemblance to *Leonardo da Vinci*, these were made entirely out of 850 tons of aluminium to reduce weight and avoid the earlier ship's stability problem. While all other seams were of a welded construction, the joins between the steel hulls and aluminium superstructures were bonded by the age-old riveting method, with a combination of synthetic rubber neoprene washers and strips to prevent corrosion of the alloy.

With the superstructure complete, work started on the most controversial and symbolic aspect of their design – the lofty, 45-foot-tall funnels. These were the result of extensive research by Professor Mortarino's team at Turin Polytechnic. Originally conceived for the new Lloyd Triestino liners, they sought the most efficient and effective method of dispersing exhaust smoke, thereby minimising the possibility of oil smuts blemishing the sprawling sun decks aft. By placing a large soot shield (early renditions show this to be oval but ultimately it was broadened aft, to create a 'wing') above a narrow

Six months after her sister's launch, *Raffaello* enters the water for the first time. Her pale hull provides a first glimpse of the liners' new livery, which was previously only found on South American and pre-war South African services. (CRDA, Italia – Alberto Imparato collection)

At Sestri Ponente, *Michelangelo*'s emerging exterior formed a vibrant dash of colour against the Genoese skyline and mountain backdrop with ochre-primed aluminium upper works topped by a red oxide steel hull, all encased in scaffold. (Ansaldo, Italia – www.michelangelo-raffaello.com)

Michelangelo's fitting out as viewed from a shipyard crane. *Leonardo da Vinci's* tiered aft decks were also part of the original design but this was changed post launch, with the Tourist Class lido extended fully to the stern, enclosing the small open promenade on the foyer deck. (Archivo Publifoto Genoa – Claudio Serra collection)

One of *Michelangelo*'s funnels takes shape. At Sestri Ponente each funnel was built piecemeal in situ. Across at San Marco, *Raffaello*'s stacks were pre-fabricated ashore and hoisted into position by the yard's huge floating crane. (Archivo Publifoto Genoa – Claudio Serra collection)

stove pipe, airflow below the shield could be optimised to create an updraft on its rear edge. This would prevent smoke from being pulled down in the vacuum generally caused by conventional funnels. Supporting the huge shield was an encircling ring of lattice work, resembling, depending upon opinion, the cage masts of pre-Second World War American battleships, or, more disparagingly, upturned wastebaskets. To traditionalists they were an anathema. Nevertheless, from a practical perspective they were effective, and like the lateral fins on *France*'s stacks, became an instantly recognisable symbol and marketing focus.

T/V MICHELANGELO
T/V RAFFAELLO

Accommodations
and characteristics of the
twin 43,000 - ton superliners

Italian Line
ITALIA — SOCIETÀ DI NAVIGAZIONE — GENOVA

Left: The funnel livery also appears to have changed at a late stage, even after *Raffaello*'s funnels were installed. As this brochure cover illustrates, the funnels initially incorporated the traditional broad red and slim white and green bands. Disappointingly, this was later amended; the resulting thinner red band became all but obscured by the shadow from the huge black soot shield. (Italian Line – Author's collection)

Below: *Michelangelo*, radiant in her freshly painted white livery, nears completion in the spring of 1965. (Archivo Publifoto Genoa – Claudio Serra collection)

Right: *Raffaello*'s looming bow. The dramatically flared design was criticised for its poor performance in heavy head seas, which resulted in the ships being rather 'stiff' sailors. (Claudio Serra collection)

Below: Italian Line publicity brochure with artist renderings of the ships and assorted public rooms. (Author's collection)

Although physically identical, the interior decoration, fixtures and fittings created ships of very different atmosphere and personality. As with *Leonardo da Vinci*, participating architects and interior designers were selected from an invitation-only competition and the same vertical class divisions prevailed. Externally the only obvious differences were in the swimming pool arrangements, particularly around the First Class lido and outer deck light fixtures.

The First Class lido provided a sheltered suntrap, augmented by infrared heat lamps. The only significant external difference between the ships was the arrangement of the swimming pools. Above is *Michelangelo*, easily identified by the white delta wing roof of the adjacent bar. Below is *Raffaello*, with the wooden circular forms. (Author's collection)

The expansive
Cabin and Tourist
Class lidos viewed
from the mainmast.
(Giancarlo
Criscuolo collection)

Internally, *Michelangelo* was regarded as the more conservative and sumptuous, being the work of (among others) Pulitzer, Monaco and Zoncada, who had also worked on *Leonardo da Vinci*, featuring deep reds, browns and black. In contrast, *Raffaello*'s fresh, bright and airy interiors incorporated paler tones, with a preponderance of blues, and had a more European feel. As well as replicating the safety features installed on *Leonardo da Vinci*, the new ships also adhered to the most stringent (Method 1) fire prevention criteria, with extensive use of British-made marinite partitioning.

First Class accommodation inevitably won plaudits for its glamour and Cabin Class for comfort. On *Raffaello* in particular design features in Cabin Class echoed those of First. Nevertheless, a trip down the stairs to Tourist Class revealed a more utilitarian atmosphere, where linoleum and plain partitioning predominated. Perhaps worst of all, even those cabins lining the ships outer plating had no natural daylight. The absurdity of not installing portholes below Cabin Deck has never been fully explained, though various reasons have been proposed; that it was a further safety feature in the wake of *Andrea Doria*, to reduce the ingress of sea water in the event of a collision, or possibly to avoid storm damage on the notorious North Atlantic. If correct, the irony of this second theory would soon reveal itself.

In early March 1965 *Michelangelo* was taken from her fitting out berth and dry docked, residual launch gear was removed and the hull was scrubbed. On 11 March, four and a half years after the first keel plate had been laid, she finally steamed out of port on preliminary builder's trials in the Gulf of Genoa. Initial satisfaction, however, became tainted by two major concerns. Veteran Ansaldo engineer Luigi Bozzo described the scene: 'Even though I continued to open the turbine steam valve, the rpm still wouldn't increase, as if something external to the ship was holding her back.' Worse still, the aft section was plagued by chronic vibration, coining the most vivid analogy from a waiter who subsequently experienced it: 'The crew dining room shakes like a harem dancer's belly.'

The tone of each ship was set in the First Class embarkation foyer. Here is *Michelangelo* showing the typically rich (and darker) Genoese red and brown tones and circular ceiling patterns of Gustavo Pulitzer Finali. Continuing the precedent set on *Leonardo da Vinci*, a silver high-relief image of the artist by goldsmith Bruno Bini is shown on the forward bulkhead. (Ansaldo, Italia – Alberto Imparato collection)

In contrast, this is the same space on *Raffaello* by Busiri-Vici, with its light feel, gold and blue hues and bas-relief portrayal of Raphael against a backdrop of St Peter's in Rome by Francesco Coccia. (CRDA, Italia – Alberto Imparato collection)

The magnificent *Fiorenze* First Class ballroom on *Michelangelo*, showing the three huge Lucite chandeliers occupying the lofty central recess and surrounding Arras tapestries. The deep red velour chairs add extra lustre. (Ansaldo, Italia – Don Leavitt collection)

The equivalent *Veneziana* ballroom on *Raffaello* by Attilio and Emilio La Padula, with the aluminium chandeliers, encircling aluminium panels and lighter tones of upholstery and carpet. These architects were responsible for many rooms in First and Tourist Class, which shared the same basic design themes. On the left is the aft bulkhead, adorned with an abstract work by Mario de Luigi. (CRDA, Italia – Don Leavitt collection)

The First Class restaurant on *Raffaello* by Michele and Giancarlo Busiri-Vici, their first ship-board commission, was a sweeping flow of fluted columns and swirling ceiling panels with incorporated lighting fixtures. Primarily white with pale blue chairs and red accents, it was one of the finest post-war dining venues afloat. (CRDA, Italia – Alberto Imparato collection)

In contrast, the rather spartan Tourist Class dining room on *Michelangelo*. (Ansaldo, Italia – Alberto Imparato collection)

The *Rosatea* (Rosemary) First Class suite on *Raffaello*. As with most express liners the top grade cabins were centrally located on a relatively low deck (in this case the boat deck) to minimise discomfort from pitching and rolling. (CRDA, Italia – Alberto Imparato collection)

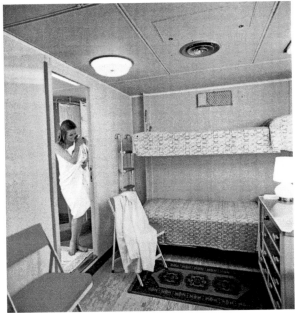

The model adds a glamorous touch to this picture of a Tourist Class cabin on *Raffaello*. Although there were private facilities in each cabin, many of those in the lowest category were small and basic, which were tolerable for emigrants in transit to the New World but hopelessly inadequate for cruise passengers sailing for fun. (Ansaldo, Italia – Alberto Imparato collection)

The three-deck-high cinema/theatre was bizarrely located high and aft (see the previous cutaway image), straddling the lido, upper and boat decks. Accommodating 489, with First Class in the balcony, this picture is of *Michelangelo*. (Giancarlo Criscuolo collection)

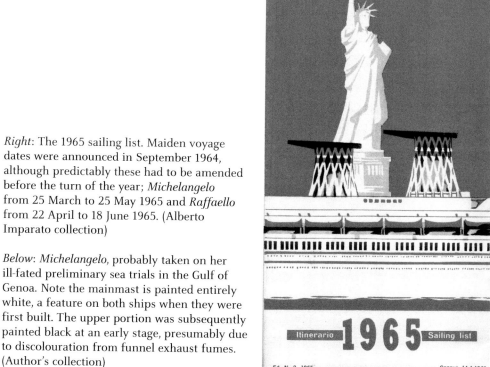

Itália NAVIGAZIONE   *Italian Line*

AL NORD AMERICA
SULLA ROTTA DEL SOLE
TO NORTH AMERICA
VIA THE SUNNY SOUTHERN ROUTE

Itinerario **1965** Sailing list

Ed. N. 2 1965   Genova 14-4-1965

Right: The 1965 sailing list. Maiden voyage dates were announced in September 1964, although predictably these had to be amended before the turn of the year; *Michelangelo* from 25 March to 25 May 1965 and *Raffaello* from 22 April to 18 June 1965. (Alberto Imparato collection)

Below: *Michelangelo*, probably taken on her ill-fated preliminary sea trials in the Gulf of Genoa. Note the mainmast is painted entirely white, a feature on both ships when they were first built. The upper portion was subsequently painted black at an early stage, presumably due to discolouration from funnel exhaust fumes. (Author's collection)

Perplexed and frustrated by their inability to find either cause or solution, Ansaldo's management sought the assistance of Nicolò Costanzi. This was an uneasy request on two counts. First, Costanzi was from Trieste and a director of Ansaldo's great shipbuilding rivals CRDA. Secondly, of course, his proposed designs for the new ships had been rejected in favour of Ansaldo's hull and machinery configuration. Setting aside any personal animosity, Costanzi set to work. After arriving in Genoa he observed the next day's trials at a distance, from a strategically placed pilot boat. Unable to conclude anything from this distant vantage point he then made a seemingly insane request. As *Michelangelo* started her next high speed run, Costanzi was lowered over her stern in a flimsy rattan basket, swaying just above the foaming wake. Back in Trieste, Costanzi analysed his observation notes and produced a report. By changing the propellers and shaft tubes he was convinced he could eliminate the problems. For *Michelangelo*, however, it was too late; with the maiden voyage already publicised and her 'shakedown' cruise planned, there was insufficient time to implement the modifications.

Meanwhile, for once the delays at San Marco proved beneficial. The 'Costanzi cure' as it was dubbed was applied to *Raffaello* prior to completion in June. No doubt it would have given the great man considerable satisfaction that over the same measured mile in the Gulf of Genoa, CRDA's charge outperformed her sister, attaining 31.5 knots and thereby becoming, briefly, the fastest Italian liner of all time (after adopting the same changes at her first dry-docking in January 1966, *Michelangelo* achieved a new record).

Heralded by whistle salutes from the adjacent *Leonardo da Vinci*, *Michelangelo* sailed on her inaugural cruise on 30 April 1965, bound for Madeira and Tenerife. As well as testing air conditioning, galley and other auxiliary equipment and machinery, it also allowed the crew time to find their way around the ship and new working environment. After returning to Genoa, provisioned and gleaming in her white livery, *Michelangelo* cast off from Ponte Andrea Doria at 11.00 on 12 May 1965, accompanied by 1,000 white doves. She was escorted through the port's narrow confines by fire boats, which were emitting fountains off each quarter, as well as numerous pleasure craft and a bevy of helicopters, including a formation from the American aircraft carrier USS *Saratoga*, which was anchored offshore.

The incumbent flagship and her successor. *Michelangelo* prepares to sail on her 'shakedown' cruise, while *Leonardo da Vinci* lies at anchor. (Alberto Imparato collection)

Above: Cadets wave a fond farewell to the departing flagship. (Archivio Publifoto Genova – Claudio Serra collection)

Below: Framed by Genoa's dramatic, terraced backdrop and escorted by celebratory fountains, *Michelangelo* sails for New York. (Archivio Publifoto Genova – Claudio Serra collection)

Earlier, among the preamble of ceremonies and the usual array of posturing politicians and dignitaries was a visit by octogenarian Elina Castellucci Buonarroti. She was the great artist/sculptor Michelangelo's last direct descendant and she emotionally presented Captain Crepaz with a family tree.

Trouble-free and placid, the new flagship's maiden crossing was a great success, with publicity film and photographs primarily concentrating on the exploits of glamorous, world renowned actress Virna Lisi. The 1,495 passengers woke to a misty morning, as *Michelangelo* sailed under the Verrazano Narrows Bridge on 20 May 1965. Accompanied by Moran tugs and fireboat spray, sunshine illuminated the Italian newcomer as she passed the Statue of Liberty, steamed up the Hudson and pirouetted into her berth at Italian Line's newly leased Pier 90.

Left: A big man with a big heart. The imposing, chiselled face of Mario Crepaz, first Captain of the *Michelangelo*. (Archivio Publifoto Genova – Claudio Serra collection)

Below: 'A dazzling gesture of faith in the future of huge passenger liners', *Michelangelo* presents a magnificent spectacle as she passes the Statue of Liberty on her maiden arrival at New York. (Peter de Monte – www. michelangelo-raffaello.com)

Dressed overall, *Michelangelo* is nudged into her slip at Pier 90, welcomed by a large contingent of New York's Italian-American community. (Theodore W. Scull)

Captain Crepaz and the aforementioned Virna Lisi offered the customary positive platitudes about the new ship to the waiting media and Mayor Robert Wagner proclaimed it 'Michelangelo Day'. The following day it was the turn of company President Giuseppe Zuccoli to talk at a formal press conference. He espoused the virtues of the new flagship, claiming she 'constituted a dazzling gesture of faith in the future of huge passenger liners and the Line's unbounded faith in the future of steamship travel'. The sentiment may have been sincere, the occasion euphoric, but in reality it was pure delusion. *Michelangelo* and *Raffaello* were the wrong ships at the wrong time; no rhetoric could change that simple fact.

Over the subsequent week the new flagship hosted various receptions for the travel press and local dignitaries. As was customary she was also opened to the inquisitive public, and 14,000 toured her public rooms. On 27 May *Michelangelo* departed New York with a healthy complement of 1,620 passengers on board – a post-war company record.

Six days later *Raffaello* left CRDA's fitting out basin and proceeded into the Adriatic for preliminary trials. After a successful introductory cruise, calling at Cannes, Malta, Piraeus and Naples, she was provisioned for her maiden transatlantic crossing.

Blessed with mid-summer sunshine and a display of medieval standard bearers from Siena, *Raffaello* cast off from Genoa at 11:00 on 26 July 1965.

Releasing a multi-coloured stream of balloons, dressed overall and with a reverberating serenade from all the ships whistles in the harbour, including *Michelangelo*, it was one of the most memorable send-offs the great port had ever witnessed. The last Italian new-build endured a rougher crossing than her sister, with wave action having stripped away some of the pristine white hull paint to reveal undercoat. Press photographs later preserved her dignity by applying liberal white touching-up to the scoured bow.

As rays of sunshine pierced the monotone grey, *Raffaello* glided up the North River on 2 August 1965 and berthed shortly after 10.00 a.m. Among the 1,121 passengers disembarking that day was the appropriately named actress Raffaella Carria, offering a glamorous touch of Italian chic to the waiting press.

Above: A vision of power and pace. On 9 June 1965, *Raffaello* arrived at Genoa for final acceptance trials, as previously mentioned achieving a higher speed at lower fuel consumption and with negligible vibration compared to her sister. (Claudio Serra collection)

Below: A beautiful postcard view of the twins illuminating the Genoa waterfront, the night before *Raffaello*'s maiden voyage to New York. (Author's collection)

Above: Streamers and cheers as *Raffaello* departs on her maiden voyage to New York. (Giancarlo Criscuolo collection)

Below: Under the watchful gaze of La Lanterna, Genoa's landmark lighthouse, *Raffaello* steams out of port. (Alberto Imparato collection)

Above: Original plans for a tandem transatlantic crossing were quietly dropped due to *Raffaello*'s delayed construction. Instead, *Michelangelo* is shown arriving on the morning of 3 August 1965 to join her sister with *United States* at Pier 86. Later *Queen Mary* and (at adjacent Pier 88) *France* were also in port, creating one of those spectacular line-ups of liners the Manhattan super piers were famous for. *Michelangelo* sailed for Europe the following day, leaving *Raffaello* to her welcoming festivities. (Italian line)

Below: In an orchestrated rendezvous, *Raffaello* was joined by *Michelangelo* on her fourth round trip crossing. This specially commissioned vinyl record cover shows the twins at Pier 90, with *Raffaello* in the foreground. (Alberto Imparato collection)

CHAPTER 3

1960–1969: Swinging between Triumph and Tribulations

Leonardo da Vinci sailing from Naples. (Ian Sebire)

While *Michelangelo* and *Raffaello* were being created and commissioned, *Leonardo da Vinci* was enjoying the most popular and profitable segment of her career. A week after her maiden arrival at New York she returned to Genoa with every berth taken, starting a short-lived but highly successful partnership with *Cristoforo Colombo* on the *linea espresso*. The new flagship's introduction coincided with the Olympic Games in Rome and she provided a special voyage aligned with the start of the XVII Olympiad on 25 August 1960. That first year *Leonardo da Vinci* undertook thirty Atlantic crossings, carrying an Italian Line record of 34,810 passengers in a twelve-month period, with a remarkable load factor (proportion of passengers to available berths) of 94 per cent.

Although the figures superficially indicated future prosperity, other events and statistics from 1960 pointed to a more sobering assessment. Similarly timed to coincide with the Roman Olympiad, Alitalia, Italy's national airline, introduced the Douglas DC-8, a four-engine inter-continental jet which reduced passage time from nine days by ship to a similar number of hours by plane. While the total number of passengers crossing the Atlantic continued to grow, the proportion crossing by ship started its inexorable decline; already it was the beginning of the end.

A serene evening at Genoa. *Leonardo da Vinci* rests at her pier in this view from 1962. (Alberto Imparato collection)

Leonardo da Vinci's cruising capability received its first test in February 1962. On the second of the month she cast off from a frigid New York on a forty-two-day Eastern Mediterranean voyage, incorporating tours to the Holy Land (from Haifa) and the Pyramids (from Alexandria), as well as exotic Istanbul, Beirut and Tangier. Carrying 498 passengers in a combined First and Cabin 'one class' configuration was close to the cruising capacity of 550. The success of this cruise led to an even more ambitious fifty-one-day itinerary for February 1963, in which she would transit the Bosporus and visit Black Sea ports.

The following year *Leonardo da Vinci* was a controversial bystander when the 7,300 grt British freighter *Ambassador* foundered in the North Atlantic. Encountering Force 10 winds and heavy seas, the 1945-built cargo ship was in a perilous condition when *Leonardo da Vinci* responded to a request for assistance at 07.30 on 18 February 1964 and sped to the scene, arriving in the early afternoon. On sighting the Italian flagship twenty men, evenly divided into two life rafts, left the heaving decks of the *Ambassador* in hope of rescue. One raft capsized, but six of the party made it safely back on board their floundering ship. The other raft drifted hopefully towards the *Leonardo da Vinci*, which had taken up station 3 miles away, but the Captain considered conditions too dangerous to launch a rescue boat and so those on board watched impotently as the ten were swept away. In the event there were twenty survivors, who were subsequently picked up by two other vessels as conditions improved. Unsurprisingly, survivors (but tellingly not the board of trade enquiry) were critical of *Leonardo da Vinci's* Captain.

When the Italian Line introduced *Michelangelo* and *Raffaello* on the *linea espresso* from Genoa in May and July 1965, *Leonardo da Vinci* switched to a more sedate schedule, home ported at Naples and sailing to New York via Genoa, Barcelona, Gibraltar and Halifax (Nova Scotia). Her itinerary

Sporting her white hull, *Leonardo da Vinci* is shown at her new home port of Naples, with the brooding presence of Vesuvius beyond. (Alberto Imparato collection)

also included periodic calls at Madeira's capital, Funchal, Casablanca, Majorca and, on the final leg, Palermo in Sicily. She operated alone, *Cristoforo Colombo* having bolstered Italia's Adriatic service from Trieste after the withdrawal of the beloved *Vulcania* and *Saturnia*. The geography of the Mediterranean, coupled with its favourable climate, meant that although still a three-class vessel, undertaking traditional liner voyages, *Leonardo da Vinci*'s eight annual round trips had a cruise-like atmosphere. The extended multi-port itinerates proved more popular than the *linea espresso*, where the superliners were fighting a futile rear-guard against the invasive jets. To homogenise the company livery, *Leonardo da Vinci* (and later *Cristoforo Colombo*) was painted with a white hull in the course of her annual dry docking in February 1966. Although the original black was smarter and the new livery highlighted each rust streak and fender scuff, it gave the ship a fresh, tropical appearance, which was particularly relevant for her increasing cruise role.

Like so many flagships before them, *Leonardo da Vinci*, *Raffaello* and *Michelangelo* attracted the patronage of stars of the silver screen, art and sport, kings of industry and even royalty and heads of state. Among the latter were the secretive Yugoslavian President Tito and King Hassan II of Morocco, accompanied by his family and fearsome bodyguard. Cinematic namedroppers were in seventh heaven, rubbing shoulders with Elizabeth Taylor and Richard Burton, Dustin Hoffman, Spencer Tracy, Alfred Hitchcock and Paul Newman as well as homegrown stars like Sofia Loren and Alberto Sordi. Representative of Italian *Alta Moda*, the ships regularly formed a backdrop to fashion shows and in 1966 three of Alfa Romeo's latest (soon to become iconic) Spider sports cars were transported to the USA. The company was seeking a novel means of introducing their car to the North American market and so one was displayed in the First Class lounge, while two more were stored and driven outdoors, 'racing' around *Raffaello*'s First Class lido.

Perhaps unfairly, *Raffaello* has always been characterised as the unlucky sister; in fact, both of the twins endured early misfortune. On 31 October 1965, less than three months into her career, *Raffaello* was steaming across the Atlantic when a crewman's momentary lapse of concentration caused heated oil to spray over an electrical control panel. The ensuing fire engulfed the aft engine room, and 90 minutes elapsed before the crew could bring the blaze under control. The damage was considerable and disabled her starboard screw and stabilisers, which caused the ship to lurch violently, resulting in fifty-six minor injuries. The split engine room configuration proved its worth and she limped on but in deteriorating conditions Captain Ribari decided to reverse course and return directly to Genoa, utilising the remaining, undamaged turbine and screw. However, worse was yet to come.

Left: Contrary to popular opinion, celebrity is not a new phenomenon, and a symbiotic relationship existed between stars and shipping lines, both benefiting from the mutual publicity. Here the German-born star of Italian cinema, Solvi Stubing, poses by an ornate midnight buffet arrangement on *Raffaello*. (Alberto Imparato collection)

Below: *Raffaello* in the Genoese dry dock of the OARN shipyard. (Archivo Publifoto Genoa – Claudio Serra collection)

On 6 April 1966, a warm spring day, *Michelangelo* departed Genoa on her regular run to New York. To the uninitiated such crossings could seem deceptively innocuous, but experienced mariners knew conditions west of the Azores were invariably tempestuous at this time of year, even on the 'Sunny Southern Route'. Six days after that benign departure *Michelangelo* was in the mid-Atlantic, lashed by hurricane force winds and monstrous seas. As a precaution Captain Soletti, on his last voyage before retirement, advised all those accommodated in cabins near the front of the ship to move further aft.

To secure a breached air intake, a party of crew members went out onto the heaving, exposed foredeck. To afford them protection from the terrifying head seas, Captain Soletti reversed course. In the deceptive lull that this induced one couple (Mr and Mrs Berndt) and a single passenger (Mr Steinback) with his accompanying servant deciding to return to their cabins at the forward end of the superstructure. They were joined by a group of young crew members, eager to witness the waves from a forward looking vantage point. It proved a fatal mistake.

Moments from disaster, 12 April 1966. *Michelangelo*'s official photographer captures images of the raging storm for posterity. (Bill Miller collection)

Michelangelo and the Wave. (Ian Sebire)

Their task complete the exhausted team clambered back inside and Captain Soletti ordered the helm over, so that *Michelangelo* was once again on course for New York and her bow to the onrushing waves. The huge ship was just completing the manoeuvre when she plunged into a particularly deep trough. Looming ahead was a vertical wall of water, estimated to be 70 feet in height. The wave engulfed the forward end of the vessel, stripping bulwarks at the prow. With its energy barely dissipated it struck the forward superstructure with an explosive impact. Such was the force generated that a portion of the forward aluminium bulkhead collapsed and a segment was peeled off, as if by some gargantuan can opener.

Above: Several of *Michelangelo*'s bridge windows were smashed when the wave struck; crew members and debris littered the floor, which was initially awash with seawater. The photograph was taken at Genoa during more tranquil times, in a lull between voyages. (Claudio Serra collection)

Left: The scene of tragedy; this photograph glimpses through the forward bulkhead ripped open by the power of the wave on the morning of 12 April. (Giancarlo Criscuolo)

Mr Steinback was killed instantly and Mr Berndt died on arrival at the hospital, although his wife survived. One young crew member, Ferrari, succumbed to his injuries.

In addition to the deaths there were several serious and superficial injuries, with the medical rooms coming to resemble a military hospital. Despite the violence of the impact, the engines, propellers and rudder were mercifully undamaged. As the storm abated *Michelangelo* gathered pace towards New York. On 15 April there was a rendezvous with a US coastguard helicopter to evacuate the most seriously injured casualty, a crew member with a fractured skull. He was winched aloft and taken to a Boston military hospital for treatment.

With her flag at half-mast, *Michelangelo* belatedly entered New York harbour on the morning of 16 April. Although a huge white tarpaulin hid her wounded superstructure, the contorted prow, missing bulwark and rust-stained hull bore testimony to her mid-Atlantic ordeal. Pier 90 was awash with traumatised relatives and an eager press corps, the latter inevitably swooping on the carrion of a tragic event. Ambulances joined taxis on the outer concourse.

Workers from the Bethlehem shipyard, across the Hudson at Hoboken, carried out temporary repairs before *Michelangelo* discreetly left Manhattan on 20 April for Genoa. Having disembarked her 870 passengers, she was then moved to the Ansaldo yard for permanent repairs, including the replacement of the buckled aluminium supporting structure by stronger steel. Testimony to the wisdom of these modifications (which were also carried out on *Raffaello*) came the following year; on 2 and 3 December 1967, *Michelangelo* encountered successive hurricane force storms, and although there were minor injuries, the ship escaped undamaged.

Highlighting perhaps the surrealism of Senior Zuccoli's remarks twelve months earlier, the superliner's results in their maiden year were predictably disappointing. Although they prompted an overall increase in passenger numbers, load factors were 63 per cent for *Michelangelo* and 70 per cent for *Raffaello*, considerably lower than their fleetmates. Crucially, although almost all their rivals – including *France*, *Bremen* and even the Cunard Queens – were engaged in off-season cruises, the Italian Line initially refused to join this seasonal migration. In July 1966 management changes prompted an abrupt volte-face.

Initially, only *Leonardo da Vinci* was assigned to take on the cruising role; meanwhile, the superliners would remain in transatlantic service, but often with additional ports of call, to provide a hybrid cruise package for those in First and Cabin Class. *Michelangelo*'s first such voyage, marketed as Mediterranean-Go-Rounds, stopped at Madeira, Tenerife, Palma de Majorca and Palermo, in addition to the usual calls at Gibraltar and Cannes. These 'Med-Go-Rounds' became an integral, popular part of the sisters' itineraries, interspersed among their express service.

Already established as the Italian Line's principal cruise ship, much of *Leonardo da Vinci*'s exceptional reputation was cemented with her long cruises to the eastern Mediterranean from New York. (Author's collection)

Above: An atmospheric panorama of Genoa at dusk. *Raffaello* lies at Ponte Andrea Doria with either *Augustus* or *Giulio Cesare* in the background and Tirrenia ferries in the foreground. (Claudio Serra collection)

Below: To broaden their appeal, extra ports were added to supplement the twins' *linea espresso* transatlantic schedules. Marketed as Mediterranean-Go-Rounds (Med-Go-Rounds) these voyages included calls at Palermo, where *Michelangelo* is shown in this wonderful scene at the Sicilian port. (Francesco Scrimali – www.michelangelo-raffaello.com)

On 1 September there was a further announcement. In addition to the Med-Go-Rounds, *Michelangelo* and *Raffaello* would join *Leonardo da Vinci* on the Caribbean circuit from early 1967. More immediately *Raffaello* undertook a first Mediterranean cruise, departing Genoa on 18 September 1966 and calling at Palma, Tripoli, Siracusa and Messina.

At noon on 8 December 1966 *Leonardo da Vinci* edged astern from New York's Pier 90, serenaded by calypso bands on Italy's first Caribbean cruise since the Second World War. The complement of 514 passengers was certainly more than would have endured a transatlantic crossing at the time. That winter witnessed *Leonardo da Vinci*'s most extensive cruise programme to date, sailing on a series of one and two-week itineraries to the Caribbean from New York until 10 February 1967.

Right: A fish-eye lens view of *Leonardo da Vinci*'s First Class lido. (Author's collection)

Below: The Italian Line persevered with year-round crossings longer than any other major shipping line. In this view, *Michelangelo* sails from a wintry Genoa with snow dusting the Liguria hillsides beyond. (Author's collection)

28-Day
PREMIÈRE
CARNIVAL IN RIO
GALA CRUISE
on the 46,000-ton luxury superliner
RAFFAELLO
from New York February 11, 1968
from Port Everglades February 13, 1968

Italian Line
THE GALA RESORT FLEET

The twins' first experience of long-distance cruising: *Raffaello*'s 'Carnival in Rio' cruise was heavily marketed and sold out in just ten weeks. (Author's collection)

In a bid to maximise passenger loads and revenue, additional ports of call were added along the Atlantic's western seaboard, as well as through the Mediterranean. On 29 May 1967 *Michelangelo* made a maiden call at Quebec and *Raffaello* stopped at Port Everglades on Boxing Day the same year. With Halifax and Boston also periodically added to the schedules, the Italian Line made every effort to broaden their appeal. Usurping Cunard as the number one transatlantic shipping carrier (in terms of passengers carried) in 1968 proved a dubious distinction, bound up more in the British line's fleet disposals than surging popularity for the 'Sunny Southern Route'. In fact given the withdrawal of rivals American Export Lines' *Independence* and *Constitution* that same year, an overall load factor of just 52 per cent (80,069 passengers from 152,259 available berths) bore witness to the overall decline. Furthermore, the trend was accelerating, with less than half the number of passengers crossing by ship in 1968 than had done so in 1965.

During this period *Raffaello* would cruise more extensively than her sister; predominantly these were to the Caribbean, sailing from New York, but on 11 February 1968 she cast off from Pier 90 and backed into a frigid Hudson on a more exotic voyage. After passing the Ambrose light she turned south, bound for the vibrant energy of Carnival in Rio. Filled to capacity the twenty-eight-day cruise incorporated calls at Port Everglades, St Thomas, Martinique, Barbados and Bahia, and then after four full days in Rio de Janeiro she returned to New York via Curacao, San Juan and finally Port Everglades. It was such a success that the itinerary was repeated by *Michelangelo* the following year.

In 1969 the twins were selected to act as mobile sets for a new movie, *My Love Help Me* (or in Italian *Amore Mio Aiutami*). Featuring Alberto Sordi and Monica Vitti, the film may be of dubious merit to English audiences, but provides a wonderful record of the ships. Somewhat indulgently public room scenes were filmed on *Raffaello* while exterior and cabin scenes came from *Michelangelo*. Garnering much-needed press attention, the film was presented for the first time on board *Michelangelo*.

Symbolic of a sea change was the magnificent sight of Italy's three largest liners, *Michelangelo*, *Raffaello* and *Leonardo da Vinci*, at adjacent Manhattan piers on 31 January 1969. All three left New York on cruises. Less poetically, but equally significant, this rendezvous was the result of yet another strike.

Intoxicating as these voyages were, they could not hide the red ink that trailed in the ships' wake. The Italian Government was already questioning its commitment to deep-sea passenger services by the end of the 1960s and in December 1969 the company made its first restructuring proposals. *Leonardo da Vinci* and *Cristoforo Colombo* would be moved to the South American La Plata service, replacing *Augustus* and *Giulio Cesare*. Whether or not this was an empty gesture to placate their political masters in Rome, it was rapidly dropped in the face of union protests.

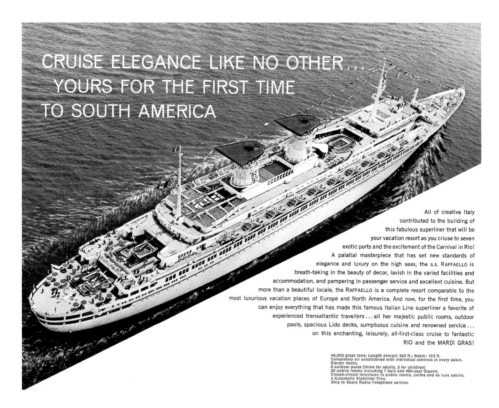

Above: Espousing the virtues of sailing on *Raffaello* for the cruise to Rio, including a superb overhead view … of *Michelangelo*. (Author's collection)

Below: Braving a chill wind on the Hudson, the photographer captures *Raffaello* and *Michelangelo* together at Pier 90 on 31 January 1969. In the distance *Leonardo da Vinci*'s mast protrudes against the Manhattan skyline. (Bill Miller collection)

CHAPTER 4

1970–1975: Cruising Towards Oblivion

Cruising into the 1970s, *Leonardo da Vinci* is seen on a shimmering sea. (Ian Sebire)

Italy endured the 'Years of Lead' (a reference to the bullets and bombs expended), as extremists of left and right resorted to violence and intimidation against the legal and political establishment. Meanwhile, the United States was blighted by Watergate, the Vietnam War, rising crime and police corruption, particularly in New York. Meanwhile, the introduction of the Boeing 747 to PAN-AM commercial service in January 1970 would revolutionise long-distance travel forever – a further nail in the coffin of the ocean liner.

Cruising had become the prime focus of *Leonardo da Vinci*'s role by the turn of the decade. The Caribbean and Mediterranean itineraries were supplemented by increasingly ambitious voyages; for example, in February 1970 she undertook a forty-one-day 'Hawaiian Paradise' voyage to Honolulu. Entering the Pacific for the first (and only) time, a highlight of this cruise was a maiden transit of the Panama Canal, including a rendezvous with Lloyd Triestino's *Guglielmo Marconi* in the Gatun Lake.

The new decade dawned inauspiciously for *Raffaello*. On the brilliantly clear, moonlit night of 19 May 1970 she passed Europa Point and made her way into Algeciras Bay, slowing as she approached the eponymous Spanish port. Departing that clear, warm night was the Norwegian tanker *Cuyahoga*. It was subsequently alleged she was travelling too fast in the tight confines of the bay. Third Officer Zichele saw *Cuyahoga*'s lights and instinctively shouted a warning; Captain Oneto immediately ordered the engines full astern but momentum kept her moving forward and at 3.38 a.m. *Raffaello*'s bow loomed

Daybreak revealed the evidence. *Raffaello* had a large 'bite' out of her bow while *Cuyahoga* had a corresponding gaping hole in a neat V on her port beam. The Italian liner made for the shipyard at Gibraltar, where repairs commenced immediately. She departed eight days later for New York but with few of the original 700 passengers on board. The majority had flown ahead. (R. Calcagno – www.michelangelo-raffaello.com)

out of the dark and struck the tanker's port side. Thankfully fears of an inferno proved unfounded, as the punctured tank was empty. *Raffaello* was hardly making headway when the collision occurred, and despite the agonising screech of contorted metal, neither vessel was in danger of sinking.

Sobering simulations later revealed that without the prompt actions of the *Raffaello*'s bridge team, and had she continued on her existing course and speed, the *Cuyahoga* would have ploughed into the liner's starboard flank, striking an area densely populated by passenger cabins. Given the hour, all would have been occupied.

The ships were already haemorrhaging lira at an alarming rate. Figures disclosed by the media suggested that Italian tax payers were subsidising passengers to the tune of $700 dollars per passage. In truth, the government was more accurately subsidising the crews and suppliers, but resentment among the general population was growing. Ironically, the shift to cruising only intensified the bitterness. Although more profitable, cruises offered none of the public service justification that could be argued for the liner route, and were predominantly filled with wealthy Americans. The ships were also handicapped by poor management decisions. *Michelangelo*'s voyage to Rio in 1969 was a case in point, where she averaged 25.39 knots (the same speed as her express crossings to Genoa). The company's insistence that their liners steamed at *tutta forza* (full power) on cruises was needlessly inefficient and simply accelerated their demise. Battered by tempestuous seas, dwindling passenger loads and sceptical politicians, *Michelangelo* and *Raffaello* especially were already on borrowed time.

Perpetual losses and government pressure forced a further reappraisal of Italian Line routes and activities. In February 1971 a new, irrational proposal was announced: the sisters would be separated, with *Raffaello* and *Leonardo da Vinci* taking over the La Plata route from the incumbent *Augustus*

Above: Photographed from the concourse of Pier 90, this October 1970 picture shows *Michelangelo*'s bow framing Cunard's *Queen Elizabeth 2*. After a troubled start the British flagship was cementing an enviable reputation and a significant proportion of transatlantic and cruise clientele. (Finn Tornquist)

Left: *Michelangelo* from above. Superficially all three ships appeared easily convertible for the cruise ship role, with their white livery, six swimming pools and 10,000 square metres of open deck. In practice too many cabins were inside and the majority of those in Tourist Class were simply too small. Their split machinery configuration and deep draught betrayed a pure liner pedigree. (Author's collection)

Above: *Leonardo da Vinci* at dusk. Combining First and Cabin Class public rooms and occupying only the best accommodation (Tourist Class was effectively unused), she developed a loyal following as a cruise ship. (Author's collection)

Below: *Raffaello* at Genoa. Like so many youngsters growing up around Genoa, Claudio Serra's experiences fostered a lifelong passion: 'In the early seventies I went with my father almost every Sunday morning to the Maritime Station. I often saw *Michelangelo* or *Raffaello* in port, preparing to sail. I listened to the Typhoon whistle every 15 minutes for 45 minutes until departure, which usually took place at about 11.15. When I got home, instead of doing my homework I would draw *Michelangelo* or *Raffaello* in a sketchbook my father bought me.' (Archivo Publifoto Genova – Claudio Serra collection)

A brochure montage of
Leonardo da Vinci aimed
at enticing prospective
cruise passengers.
(Author's collection)

and *Giulio Cesare*, while *Michelangelo* remained on the North Atlantic with *Cristoforo Colombo*. Mismatching ships of incompatible size and speed made no commercial sense and the plans were quietly dropped amid more vociferous union protests. However, the intent was clear; changes were required. The original schedules for 1971 advertised twenty-eight Atlantic crossings by the twins (including three 'Med-Go-Rounds') and twelve cruises, but this was subsequently altered to an equal number (twenty-two) of crossings and cruises. A new and highly popular $150 student fare was introduced, attracting a fresh, young American clientele keen to explore Europe on a budget as well as young liner buffs desperate to experience liner travel before it disappeared forever.

In January 1972 *Leonardo da Vinci* departed the Big Apple on a fifty-one-day 'African Safari' cruise – the Italian Line's first foray to southern Africa since the pre-war liner service. After calling at Martinique, passengers made their first landfall on the continent at Senegal, before moving on to Sierra Leone and Angola on the eastern seaboard. From Luanda she steamed south, skirting the Namibian coast before the most eagerly anticipated calls at Cape Town and Durban in South Africa. Sated from safari's and visits to the Stellenbosch vineyards, *Leonardo*'s passengers crossed the South Atlantic via remote Tristan da Cunha to Rio de Janeiro and Bahia in Brazil before returning to New York via Puerto Rico and St Thomas.

A couple of months later *Leonardo da Vinci* garnered unwanted attention on a rare westbound crossing. While steaming mid-ocean, the Italian Line's New York office received a ransom demand for $100,000. The anonymous caller claimed that a bomb had been planted in an unspecified location on board that would be detonated unless his demands were met. A delegation of crew members were despatched to search the ship but there was no panic and no device was found. Only a week before,

54

Above: *Leonardo da Vinci* sails from Genoa. (Claudio Serra collection)

Right: The 1973 programme saw a further reduction in Atlantic crossings by the sisters, with just twenty-one round trips planned (including five Med-Go-Rounds) and thirty-one cruises. (Alberto Imparato collection)

Italian Line
1973 CARIBBEAN CRUISES

bomb disposal experts had parachuted into the Atlantic to save the *QE2* after a similar demand had been received. This unimaginative desperado had clearly tried to replicate the plan.

Michelangelo undertook one of the longest cruises of her career in January 1973, departing the Big Apple on 4 January. With the famed Piers 90 and 88 in the process of redevelopment, she moored up at a rather ramshackle Pier 86, the former United States Lines' berth, on her return twenty-eight days later. On 4 February there was a nostalgic reunion as *QE2* joined her at Pier 86 and *France* was tethered to adjacent Pier 84. Perhaps symbolical, it was a drab, drizzly day; although reminiscent of the great line-ups from yesteryear, it was more appropriately a maritime death row, with two of the three on suspended sentences, and at that stage even *QE2*'s future in doubt.

The first timetable for the dissolution of the entire FINMARE fleet was presented to parliament on the last day of February 1973. Minister for the Merchant Marine, Giuseppe Lupis, proposed legislation that all deep-sea passenger services be terminated by 1978.

In August 1973 Italia announced several changes for the forthcoming year. Not before time it was decided to drop the outmoded three-class system by eliminating Cabin Class. Reconfigured accordingly, *Leonardo da Vinci* offered accommodation for 359 (plus a possible 244 upper berths) First Class and 681 Tourist Class passengers, while *Michelangelo* and *Raffaello* offered 843 (158 upper berths) in First and 681 in Tourist. To increase revenue the twins' cruise capacity was increased to 1,400 and all crossings would call at Lisbon and Barcelona, thus extinguishing the last vestiges of the *linea espresso*.

With the inevitability of impending withdrawal hanging over them the *coup de grâs* came in October 1973 with the OPEC oil crisis. To gain immediate economies the additional calls at Barcelona, Lisbon and Madeira were dropped from November 1973, but nine-day crossings maintained, at a more sedate and fuel efficient 22 knots. A 20 per cent fuel surcharge was also introduced. Cost, however, was not the only issue; on 5 January 1974 *Michelangelo*'s departure from Genoa to New York was cancelled at short notice due to the unavailability of fuel in the United States.

It was too late perhaps, but changes were made to *Leonardo da Vinci*'s itineraries in an attempt to reduce costs and increase revenue. From March to May 1974 the Caribbean cruise season migrated from New York to Port Everglades, saving both fuel and inclement passage time along the eastern seaboard.

Meanwhile, the sister ships were heading for pastures new. On 26 July 1974 *Michelangelo* cast off from Genoa on a cruise that would take her the length of the continent. Departing late in the morning she called briefly at Cannes that afternoon before making for Alicante, where she arrived the following day. Having rounded Punta de Taira on the continent's southern tip, she headed north-west to Lisbon. On 1 August 1974, the 45,000-ton liner became the largest and longest passenger ship to sail up the Thames, mooring at the famed Tilbury landing stage. Having sampled the delights of England's capital city during an overnight stay, *Michelangelo* steamed north, skirting the Scottish and Norwegian coastlines into the Arctic Circle, to North Cape and the roof of Europe. Inclement weather prevented her scheduled call at Hammerfest, so passengers had to be content with a sea level view of the continent's northernmost point. Returning via Norway's medieval capital, Trondheim, and the iconic Geirangerfjord, she called at Bergen and then, on successive days, Oslo and Copenhagen. From the Baltic she steamed south to Genoa via the Iberian ports of Vigo and Barcelona. The cruise proved very popular and planning commenced for *Raffaello* to undertake a similar itinerary in the summer of 1975.

While *Michelangelo* had been venturing to the Arctic, *Raffaello* was in the Eastern Mediterranean giving her passengers the opportunity to visit exotic antiquities from Alexandria, Haifa and Istanbul. *Michelangelo* also visited this region in 1974, steaming through the Bosporus to call at Sochi. These grand escapades could not, however, mask the underlying discontent. Bookings on the company's North America service were down by over 30 per cent and even the cruise activity had proportionally diminished. It is alleged that some of this was due to an unwritten agreement among American travel agents to promote the interests of rival lines. Enquiring passengers were told the Italian liners were filled when in fact they had plenty of capacity. Closer to home the government came under pressure

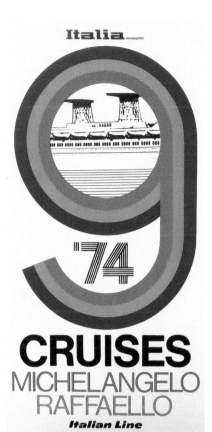

Right: While the North American cruise schedules remained largely predictable, there were innovative itineraries devised for cruises from Genoa. (Author's collection)

Below: *Michelangelo* reflected in the clear, still waters of Geirangerfjord in the course of her North Cape cruise. (Author's collection)

The *Michelangelo* near Drøbak in Oslofjord on 10 Aug 1974. Uwe Jespersen describes the scene of this ethereal picture: 'It was very early in the morning. I was actually sleeping on the cliff so as not to be late, and woke to a slightly misty dawn. I heard the most magical sound of a trumpet solo in the distance, quite inexplicable to begin with. I later found out that a nearby naval station held nice tradition in high regard. They probably still do, I guess. I loved it, it felt almost spiritual. Minutes later the stately liner glided into view, faintly humming.' (itsfoto)

from private operators, who complained that the subsidised Italian Line vessels had an unfair competitive advantage in cruises sailing out of Italian ports.

Throughout this period mutual animosity characterised pay and condition negotiations, with strikes a persistent feature of the passenger ship experience. Initially the Italian Line was ready to compromise, but unions and management became ever more entrenched and isolated. Matters came to a head following the oil crisis of 1973. With crude oil, the other principle operating cost, quadrupling in price, the Italian Line was forced to apply for a substantial increase in its annual subsidy.

1975 dawned with an ominous air of inevitability. Schedules included thirty-one crossings, four Med-Go-Rounds and thirty-three cruises. It was hoped that a designated Vatican 'Holy Year' might draw an increased clientele, together with sea-going devotees who had lost *France* the previous autumn. In fact it was pure fantasy.

No doubt Italian Line board members in Genoa and ministers in Rome closely monitored events in neighbouring France in the late summer of 1974. Exasperated by the cost of maintaining their national flagship in service, the French Government ceased all subsidy, prompting her withdrawal from service. Even a mutiny failed to reverse the decision and *France* was abruptly decommissioned. (Author's collection)

Italian Line

Transatlantic voyages to/from the Mediterranean

1975 rates

SS MICHELANGELO • SS RAFFAELLO • SS LEONARDO DA VINCI

A magical scene of *Michelangelo* illuminated at Pier 90 in front of the Empire State building on the cover of the 1975 transatlantic schedules. In fact, by this time the ships were utilising the redeveloped finger piers. (Author's collection)

CHAPTER 5

1975–1976: The End of the Line

A beautiful picture of the twins at Genoa. Uwe Jespersen recalls: 'I researched a little prior to the arrival of the *Michelangelo* to find out where to go and took a cab to the location I chose. The cabby was, shall we say, a little apprehensive when we got there, somewhere in a godforsaken spot in the port of Genoa, and I asked him to just wait. He found the whole situation rather dubious I suppose, but he did get very excited and proud though, once the *Michelangelo* arrived and made the picture possible. It was a great moment.' (itsfoto)

On 24 March 1975, *Leonardo da Vinci* cast off from Port Everglades on 'Grand Cruise '75', a fifty-day, sixteen-port odyssey to Istanbul and the Eastern Mediterranean via the Caribbean. Any sense of euphoria was quickly dispelled the following day as the government announced that all of FINMARE's deep-sea passenger services (Italian Line and Lloyd Triestino) were to be phased out by the end of 1977, with subsidies being cut accordingly. Almost immediately the Italian Line announced its programme of dismemberment. As the greatest drain on resources, *Michelangelo* and *Raffaello* would be withdrawn as soon as practicable, and *Leonardo da Vinci* by the end of 1976.

On 21 April 1975, having returned to New York from a Caribbean cruise, a rust-streaked *Raffaello* eased out into the Hudson at the start of her 226th and final transatlantic crossing. With less than a decade of service her departure seemed almost furtive, although a crowd of well-wishers populated the end of Pier 86 and the crew of the adjacent Holland-America *Ryndam* lined the rails in admiration. Nine days later she arrived at Genoa, and after disembarking her 835 passengers, crew members started stripping her artwork and removing stores. On 6 June she left Genoa and anchored in the shelter of Portovenere Bay, ominously close to the scrapyards of La Spezia.

In contrast to *Raffaello*'s relative anonymity, *Michelangelo* was afforded a heartfelt send off on 26 June 1975, on her final New York departure. Bedecked with flags, she exchanged whistle salutes with the adjacent *Kungsholm* before edging out into the Hudson. As she sailed downriver accompanied by fountains of fireboat spray, passengers lined the rails and waved a melancholic farewell. The infamous Wallis Simpson, Duchess of Windsor, was among the 1,202 on board. Like *Michelangelo*, this would be her last Atlantic crossing.

The final evening's gala dinner was followed by a heartrending ceremony where a large sugar model of the ship was symbolically slipped over the side and dissolved into the brine. Once again with flags from stem to stern, because as Captain Cosulich observed, 'it is customary to dress a corpse at a funeral', *Michelangelo* slipped into Genoa on the afternoon of 5 July 1975. Swiftly divested of her artwork, the deposed national flagship was moved to Calata Zingari, Genoa, for laying up.

As though anchored on a cruise, *Raffaello* is seen at Portovenere. Alberto Imparato was a young boy living in the village of San Terenzo (where the poet Shelley lived and died). He recalls his father taking him on a boat trip to see the great liner: 'After half an hour we were alongside the ship. Slowly we did a circumnavigation, I was struck by the stern with the double layer of verandas and the 'Beware of propellers' sign. The immense white hull was already flecked with rust while the long row of Promenade Deck windows reflected the cobalt sky.' (Alberto Imparato collection)

Alberto Imparato continues: 'I was frightened as we moved under the bow, just one metre from the cutwater. Then I saw the name *Raffaello* and those magical trellis funnels. Above them was the Italian flag. Many years have passed since then but I remember with nostalgia that was the first time I felt proud to be Italian.' (Hugh Llewellyn)

A classic promotional view of *Michelangelo*; soon such scenes would just be memories as the sun set on the ships careers. (Alberto Imparato collection)

Rumours abounded regarding the sisters' fates. Knut Kloster was one of several prominent ship owners who inspected them for potential cruise service. Greek, Italian and even Soviet interests also looked, but came to the same conclusion. The shortcomings of design, too many inside cabins and the split engine room configuration would prove too costly to rectify. Yet, they may have had a worthy and fulfilling afterlife if a combination of media pressure and political pride had not intervened. On 17 September 1975 reports suggested both ships had been sold to a Liechtenstein-based company, G. Tronado, for conversion into cancer clinics, offering a combination of treatment and recuperation. The $25 million sale was ultimately vetoed by the government after an outcry that such a role was demeaning for the vessels, despite the fact that the organisation intended to retain Italian crews and award the conversion contract to an Italian yard.

By the end of the year onward sale for further trading had been largely abandoned as the focus shifted to a static role. With American and Arab investors prominent, bids were submitted but no agreement was reached. On 15 September 1976 *Michelangelo* left Genoa under tow. Her portside lifeboats had been removed and the reason soon became evident; as *Michelangelo* was to join her sister at Portovenere, *Raffaello*'s starboard lifeboats had been removed and the two ships were tethered stem to stern, as though conjoined.

Ironically, in the short term the withdrawal of *Raffaello* and *Michelangelo* offered a reprieve, as well as promotion for *Leonardo da Vinci*. By the end of June 1975 she was restored as the national flagship, taking over the superliners' cruise itineraries, including a first foray to Northern Europe. On 24 July 1975 *Leonardo da Vinci* departed Genoa bound for Vigo and Dublin en route to Bergen, the fjords and ultimately the North Cape. From the scenic splendours of Norway she sailed to Iceland before heading south to Lisbon and then home. Crossings were now merely positioning voyages between Mediterranean and Caribbean cruises.

The twins at Portovenere. Alberto Imparato recalls: 'After a couple of false starts *Michelangelo* arrived on the morning of 16 September 1976, the day I went back to school after the summer holidays. When I looked out at 7 a.m. *Michelangelo* was surrounded by tugs. The manoeuvres were very slow and lasted until about 1 p.m. It was a terrible thing; *Raffaello* alone looked alright but the two ships tethered bow to stern was ugly to see. Often still when I look towards Portovenere I think of those two ships.' (Alberto Imparato collection)

Left: *Leonardo da Vinci*'s summer cruises advertisement for 1976. (Alberto Imparato collection)

Below: Restored as flagship of the Italian merchant marine, *Leonardo da Vinci* enters Piraeus harbour during an Eastern Mediterranean cruise. This view was taken from the *Vistafjord*. (itsfoto)

As the Italian Line fleet was systematically dismembered, crew morale evaporated. The malaise resulted in poor external maintenance, unkempt interiors and shoddy service, especially in Tourist Class. *Leonardo da Vinci*'s planned final year commenced with an Eastern Mediterranean cruise, before crossing to New York in mid-January for a series of Caribbean cruises. After the annual spring Mediterranean voyage she was back cruising from the USA at the beginning of May. On 27 June 1976 the rust-streaked ship commenced what was due to be her last scheduled transatlantic crossing from a disinterested Manhattan. Looking rejuvenated from a fresh coat of white paint, she then sailed from Naples on a series of European cruises, including one to the Scandinavian capitals, which saw a maiden call at Southampton.

Rather than being de-stored and laid up on her return to Naples at the end of September, she embarked passengers for a crossing to New York and a further season of Caribbean cruises. It was a misguided, desperate attempt to keep the last viable cruise ship in the Italian Line's fleet sailing, however poor bookings and escalating costs brought about a premature end. On 25 March 1977 *Leonardo da Vinci* edged away from the redeveloped Manhattan finger piers, and with 850 passengers on board steamed out of New York on her and the company's final transatlantic crossing.

The drama of departure. Scarred with rust but still impressive, *Leonardo da Vinci* backs out into the Hudson at the start of another voyage. (William H. Miller)

CHAPTER 6

1977–1991: ICI, Iran, and Indignity

Charred and contorted, the once elegant funnel and upper decks of *Leonardo da Vinci* protrude above the waters off La Spezia. (Alberto Imparato collection)

As part of a government initiative to re-employ elements of the FINMARE fleet, an amalgam of Italian shipping lines formed Italia Crociere Internazionali (ICI) in April 1977. Theoretically it was a sound idea; the Caribbean cruise trade was booming and the state would pay to convert its superannuated tonnage into one-class cruise ships, which the private companies within the conglomerate could use their superior marketing and commercial experience to operate. Doubtless heeding the opinion of would-be competitors, *Michelangelo* and *Raffaello* were excluded from the project as the conversion costs were simply too high. *Leonardo da Vinci* was refitted, however, and chartered by Costa Line on a three-year deal.

Symptomatic of ICI's dysfunctional complexity was the new funnel livery, which incorporated a large Costa 'C' with FINMARE's anchor over the original Italian Line red, white and green bands. *Leonardo da Vinci* repositioned to Port Everglades for three- and four-day jaunts to the Bahamas (Nassau and Freeport), where initial results were quite promising. Over the winter of 1977 she received a further refit but within a year the agreement had been terminated. Costa management were appalled at her astronomic fuel consumption; reportedly she burned more oil in port than fleetmate *Flavia* did when at sea. An almost literal white elephant, she returned to Italy, and on 23 September 1978 joined a moribund assortment of vessels close to the scrapyards of La Spezia.

Above: An official Italian Cruises International postcard with the logo superimposed on *Leonardo da Vinci*'s funnel. The original photograph dates from 1970 as she sails under the 'Bridge of the Americas' during her one and only transit of the Panama Canal. (Author's collection)

Right: An ICI brochure for *Leonardo da Vinci*. Although still sailing, it was a rather dubious 'booze cruise' existence for the former flagship of the Renaissance fleet. (Author's collection)

Italian Cruises International

Effective Apr. 1978

TS **LEONARDO DA VINCI**

Freeport/Nassau

3 AND 4 DAY CRUISES
FROM
FT. LAUDERDALE
FLORIDA

Italian Registry, Crew, Service

Meanwhile, *Michelangelo* and *Raffaello* had finally been sold. Their purchaser, for $35 million, was by the Imperial Iranian Navy – a customer that evidently met the Italian Government's self-imposed suitability criteria. The Iranian Navy intended to use the vessels as floating barracks and the terms of the sale included upgrades to the water distillation and air conditioning equipment for their new role. Amidst predictable pomp and ceremony the contract was signed in Tehran on 12 December 1976. On 18 January 1977 *Michelangelo* was towed to OARN for conversion while *Raffaello* went to the Cantieri del Tirreno yard for similar work.

Proudly still flying the Italian flag, although with her funnel livery painted out *Michelangelo* departed Genoa to a crescendo of whistle salutes on 8 July 1977. Having crossed the Mediterranean, she made a maiden transit of the Suez Canal and entered the Indian Ocean. After skirting the Yemeni coast, she passed through the notorious Straits of Hormuz, and thirteen days after leaving Genoa arrived at Bandar Abbas, Iran's premier naval base. In a formal ceremony performed in front of Shah Rezhi Pahlevi, Iran's ensign was raised, replacing its Italian counterpart. Just over a month later *Raffaello* made the same voyage east and briefly joined her sister for a final time before making her way up the Persian Gulf to the port of Bushire. As part of the sale contract a small contingent of Italian crew members were assigned to each vessel, working four-month cycles and providing maintenance and advice to Iranian counterparts.

Ironically the ship's three-class accommodation was perfectly suited to the new role. Officers (including in several cases their families) enjoyed the capacious First Class cabins and public rooms. Non-commissioned officers were placed in Cabin Class while ratings were billeted in Tourist Class. The latter, often conscripts from rural communities, were ill at ease in the liners' alien environment and frequently took their meals sitting cross legged on deck rather than in the designated dining room with unfamiliar cutlery and bone china service.

There were echoes of their transatlantic heyday with parties in the First Class ballrooms attended by Tehran's social elite, including the Shah himself. In 1978 there was even consideration given to reactivating both vessels as one-class cruise ships, to be renamed *Reza Shah the Great* and *Cyrus the*

Michelangelo undergoing conversion for her new role in the Persian Gulf. Externally both ships received a much needed coat of paint and stanchions proliferated across all open deck space, supports for awnings designed to provide essential shade from the intense Arabian sun. Internally a laundry was installed in one of the redundant public rooms. (Marc-Antoine Bombail)

Great. In concept it was as deluded as Iran's failing regime, which was overthrown by the Islamic Revolution in 1979. Suddenly the former Italian superliners found themselves abandoned, the Italian crews isolated and fearful. Rats replaced ratings in the corridors and both ships were pillaged. Ayatollah Khomeini's government defaulted on their maintenance contract as western sanctions were imposed, and so midway through 1980 the Italian crews returned home. They were not replaced.

Back in Italy, *Leonardo da Vinci* became the subject of numerous projects for regeneration. Although only eighteen years old, she was effectively from another era, and despite the ICI refit needed radical changes to make her a viable cruise ship. American investors wanted her as a floating casino, the Chinese allegedly showed interest, and there was a plan from London businessmen to moor her on the Thames as a floating hotel. Meanwhile, she was costing $2,000 a day to keep in lay-up and in June 1979 was slightly damaged by a fire on board the adjacent, redundant, cargo liner *Da Recco*. In the autumn of 1979 a firm proposal was made by Trident Corporation to restore her as a luxury cruise ship, retaining her name but controversially operating with an international crew under the Panamanian flag. Political sensibilities once again intervened. Under pressure from unions, the government blocked the sale, pending a resolution of the crew and flagging concerns. Retaining Italian jobs and control were deemed essential, although neither would materialise without a new owner.

Ultimately it all proved academic. As negotiations went on, *Leonardo da Vinci* continued to languish and deteriorate until the afternoon of 3 July 1980. It started in the chapel; a spark, a flame. Without means or manpower on board to halt its progress, the fire spread rapidly, engulfing the ship despite the valiant efforts of local firefighting tugs. With morbid curiosity, crowds lined the La Spezia shoreline. Meanwhile, conscious that she still held almost 2,000 tons of oil in her bunkers, the authorities decided to tow her out of the anchorage and scuttle the forlorn *Leonardo* in deeper water. Those once sparkling white flanks blistered and browned, the searing heat contorting her upper works into a grotesque twisted disfigurement. Thwarted in their attempts to sink her on an even keel, she listed to starboard, replicating *Andrea Doria*'s death throws, before settling on her side, with the once elegant mast detached and buckled.

Alberto Imparato recalls the scene: 'The ship was towed outside the breakwater. She burned for three days and I remember the air was unbreathable. Sometimes we had to stay inside with the windows closed because it was raining ash; perhaps it was also asbestos unfortunately! When on Sunday 6 July 1980 the ship sank around 1.30 p.m., I remember she swayed and then gradually slumped on her side, a really sad sight. I saw people in tears who I then knew to be old mariners. It was like when you see a person in your family that slowly suffers and then dies.' (Alberto Imparato collection)

Above: Conspiracy theories abounded that arson was the cause, nourished by the declaration that she was insured for over $7 million but worth only $1.1 million in scrap value. The hulk was raised and towed to La Spezia, where dismembering commenced in May 1982. (Alberto Imparato collection)

Below: The sinking of *Raffaello*. Accounts vary but the consensus is that she was struck by at least two weapons, which are believed to have been a torpedo and a missile. With smoke billowing from her aft decks, the crippled *Raffaello* was attacked again the following day, when further damage was inflicted. Whether it was a result of this Iraqi sortie or whether she was deliberately scuttled, the end result was fatal and *Raffaello* sank into the shallow waters off Bushire. (Ian Sebire)

Meanwhile, in Iran, unkempt and unwanted *Michelangelo* and *Raffaello* deteriorated rapidly. Soon their situation became even more perilous with the advent of the Iran-Iraq War of 1980. Although Iranian forces rebuffed the Iraqi invasion, Saddam Hussain's air force launched repeated attacks on military and infrastructure targets. *Raffaello* was in particular danger as Bushire was adjacent to the large oil complex at Kharg and close to Iran's aborted nuclear power plant facility. The rust-streaked white behemoth was a landmark for approaching aircraft and so she was towed to a point approximately 1 kilometre offshore.

In a morbid re-enactment of the culling of the former Italian flagship *Rex* in September 1944, Iraqi bombers swept in across the Gulf waters as dawn approached on 20 November 1982. Although their main targets were tankers moored at Kharg (two of which were sunk), the huge and defenceless *Raffaello* represented an easy prize.

Bandar Abbas was out of range for the Iraqi Air Force and so *Michelangelo* avoided her sister's fate, but the intense tropical sun and negligent authorities soon destroyed any reprieve from her steady decay. There were further rumours of an impending sale to Premier Cruises for Caribbean service, but predictably it came to nothing.

In August 1986 both ships were offered for sale, *Michelangelo* for $3 million and the wreck of the *Raffaello* $2 million. *Michelangelo* was reputedly sold to Taiwanese breakers in 1987, but this fell through. That same year, on 4 March, *Raffaello* made news when the sunken liner was struck by the freighter *Iran Salam*, severely damaging the cargo ship.

Having spent more than half her existence languishing in decrepit limbo, *Michelangelo*'s end finally came in 1991. Stripped of her superstructure to reduce the draught, the hulk departed Bandar Abbas under tow and arrived off Gadani Beach, Pakistan, on 6 June 1991. Two days later she was run up onto the gently shelving, oil-stained sands, where local Pathan tribesmen, employed by Ghaffar Dada shipbreakers, commenced the manual dismembering of Italia's erstwhile flagship. By the end of the year she was gone.

Despite various plans, the former *Raffaello* has never been salvaged. She lies on the seabed at 28° 49 minutes and 0.24 seconds north, 50° 52 minutes and 36.58 seconds east, pillaged by trophy-hunting divers and overgrown by marine organisms. Photographs show a spectral vessel, lost in a marine catacomb. A collection of white buoys mark the wreck.

The remains of *Michelangelo* are dismembered at Gadani Beach, Pakistan, in 1991. (Ian Sebire)

71

CHAPTER 7

Life On Board

Welcome aboard! (Giancarlo Criscuolo)

Any appraisal of the passenger experience on board the Italian Line's final three flagships necessarily requires a distinction between those embarking on a liner voyage and those going cruising.

Exotic ports of call have always been part of the cruise ship experience. Here *Raffaello* is seen at Casablanca. (Giancarlo Criscuolo)

Passenger Experience – Cruises

Cruises by definition are a circular experience; a shipboard holiday that in the 1960s and early 1970s was primarily, though not exclusively, the preserve of the rich and elderly. With relatively few exceptions, they departed from New York. Week-long sojourns to the Caribbean included two or sometimes three ports of call, requiring the ships to steam at full service speed down the eastern seaboard. Boarding and daily life was an altogether more leisurely experience, and with the passenger complement restricted to about 850 on the *Leonardo da Vinci* and 1,000 on the *Michelangelo* and *Raffaello*, each ship felt more spacious.

The company offered a wide variety of organised tours and experiences, and on the more exotic voyages invariably included overnight stays. As the cruises got longer the average age increased, so that a forty-two-night voyage to the eastern Mediterranean was invariably undertaken with a full complement of septuagenarians and octogenarians – the only people with the time and wealth for such an indulgence. As well as age there was also a direct correlation between the length of voyage and passenger expectation. The highest standards of service were demanded and provided as those longer cruises developed a clubby feel in which a social elite prevailed.

Of the three ships *Leonardo da Vinci* was undoubtedly the most popular. An intangible quality pervaded the ship, a happy combination of attentive crew, elegant public rooms and indulgent itineraries. Somehow the twins never attained the same popularity and results, although each had their followers.

Passenger Experience – Linea Espresso

Crossings created a special atmosphere, which was evident even before getting on board. Travelling from A to B was a comma, an interlude punctuating another goal, whether on business, visiting friends and family, undertaking a European or North American holiday or, even in the 1960s, starting a new life on a different continent. Embarkation, particularly at the terminal ports (Genoa and Naples in Italy and

Michelangelo and *Raffaello* together at Genoa. Despite appearances this was a melancholic moment; *Raffaello* is laid up prior to removal to Portovenere Bay, while *Michelangelo* will be preparing for her penultimate crossing. (itsfoto)

New York in the USA), was a noisy, often chaotic affair. For regular travellers, predominantly in First or Cabin Class, there was detached acceptance, but to the uninitiated, particularly in Tourist Class, the heady mix of apprehension, excitement and ignorance could result in animated discussions with family and officials. Many would already have been travelling for hours, if not days.

Officials in every port could be generously helpful, overtly officious or in certain cases openly unscrupulous. Richard Volpe's recollection of getting his car on board at Naples is probably not an isolated case, amusing in hindsight but not at the time:

After getting up a 3:30 a.m. and driving from Rome to Naples, we were at the dock in Naples by 9:00 a.m. Amy went on board to make sure everything was alright with our room while I began what would be the most interesting set of negotiations I ever encountered, trying to get our car on board. To make a long story short, at 11:50 a.m., 10 minutes before sailing, I saw the tail lights of my BMW disappear through the garage doors of the *Michelangelo*. The negotiations were with the dock workers. In Naples, nothing moves unless you take care of the people in charge. At first, the person in charge of loading the car told me he did not speak English and he could not understand any of my Italian. After handing him several hundred lira, miraculously he could understand my Italian and, amazingly, his English improved also. Getting all the papers signed and talking to all the necessary people took an agonisingly long period of time. Every person I spoke to had the same problem understanding me but when I produced some lira the communication problem ended. Remember, I started this process before 9:00 a.m. and I finally got the car on the ship at about 11:50 a.m., only 10 minutes before the scheduled sailing time. When I drove the car up the ramp to the garage door of the *Michelangelo*, I had to get out and let a crew member from the ship drive it into the garage. When I got out I was told by the dock worker standing on the top of the ramp that I was missing a signature on one of the documents, so he would not release the car. The Italian Line crew member heard this and he immediately began a heated argument with the dock worker in Italian. They were speaking so fast (and loud) that I could not understand all of it but I understood enough to realise that the crew member, on my behalf, told him in the first place the signature was not required, and secondly they had extorted enough money from me. He then pushed the dock worker aside, told me to go on board via the passenger ramp and drove the car into the ship. The crew member did not request a tip. I attempted to find him later after I boarded in order to thank him for his assistance, but I never saw him again. It was a most interesting morning.

Added to the mix was a small army of well-wishers (frequently outnumbering actual passengers) who swarmed on board, ostensibly to wish their traveller 'buon viaggio' but also to nose around the vessel and enjoy whatever party fare was on offer. While the passengers were funnelled on board, the crew were taking on final provisions, those mind-boggling statistics so beloved of the media and passengers: 20 tons of meat; 20 tons of milk and a further 20 tons of fresh vegetables; 5 tons of lobsters and fish; and 76,000 eggs. Lubrication was ensured thanks to the 10,500 bottles of wine (plus 3,000 bottles of champagne) stored in the cellars and over 16,000 quarts of beer in special tanks.

Bustling around the disconcerting labyrinth of the lower decks laden with cases and associated paraphernalia, novice Tourist Class travellers would ultimately – and probably after a number of false starts – find their cabin and home for the next week. Up above, having entered via their own spacious lobbies, those occupying First and Cabin Class would be settling into their luxurious suites and cabins. As sailing time drew near (11.00 from Genoa, midday from New York), the ship's whistle boomed out 15-minute alarm calls and loud speakers broadcast the warning to visitors, 'La nave è in partenza' ('The ship is about to sail'), prompting involuntary stowaways to depart and passengers to make their way to the outer decks. The scene was awash with emotion as the great liner almost imperceptibly edged away from the quay, prompting waving handkerchiefs and inaudible calls ashore and afloat.

With the theatre of departure concluded, everyone settled into the rhythm of shipboard life. For westbound passengers there was the distraction of early ports of call, initially at Cannes (5 to 6 hours after casting off from Genoa) for an hour or two, to embark passengers from tenders and limousines from attendant barges.

A *buon viaggio* party on board *Leonardo da Vinci*. The picture is taken in New York and United States Line's Pier 86 can be glimpsed through the window, which dates this publicity photograph early in the ship's career, when the Italian Line utilised Pier 84. (Author's collection)

A magnificent photograph showing the activity swarming around a recently arrived liner; *Michelangelo* at Naples in 1969. (Theodore W. Scull)

At Naples the following morning, the ship stayed several hours, allowing interested parties the opportunity to visit the city or neighbouring antiquities of Pompeii or Herculaneum. The next call was Gibraltar, a further day on and like Cannes a brief 'technical call' in the anchorage to embark/disembark a handful of passengers.

For those travelling east, landfall was five days away, and once their ship had skirted Long Island and steamed past the Ambrose Light, she then set course for the Azores and the Mediterranean.

A mix of American and Italian films were run in the cinema/theatre on a repeated cycle through the day. The confusing spectacle of American teenage audiences eagerly attending the Italian screenings was explained by the uncensored scenes of nudity in some continental films. More cerebral daytime pursuits included bridge drives, language lessons, dance classes or a cookery demonstration.

For the active, each vessel had a gym incorporating contemporary equipment, which appear quaintly bizarre by today's hi-tech standards.

Many, however, will concur with Richard Volpe's observation: 'Just sitting in a deck chair on the enclosed promenade deck and reading a book while looking out at the rolling sea was a treat.' The time-honoured pleasures of chatting, people watching and ocean gazing on a sun-drenched lido or cocooned on the enclosed promenade passed many hours at sea.

The legendary Italian love of family and children was always evident. Andrew Bryant recalls:

It was a truly magical experience, even for a nine year old. My brother James and I would take 'penny' tours of the ship, by flipping a coin whenever we came to a juncture – heads we went left or up, tails we went right or down. From First Class we ventured into both Cabin and Tourist Classes, and even in to the crew areas. Total freedom for us – it was wonderful.

Right: An early issue postcard, *Leonardo da Vinci* approaches Gibraltar on her maiden voyage to New York. (Author's collection)

Below: A classic postcard view of *Michelangelo* on the Hudson River with the Manhattan skyline, including the Empire State building, beyond. (Author's collection)

T/n Leonardo da Vinci - Gibilterra

ACTIVITIES OF THE DAY
S/S LEONARDO DA VINCI

2nd Day at Sea

6:00 A.M.	COFFEE SERVED FOR THE EARLY BIRDS—Lido Bar (Lido Deck)
7:30-9:30 A.M.	BREAKFAST—Capri and Tivoli Restaurants (Foyer Deck)
10:00 A.M.	OPEN AIR EXERCISES for beauty and health.
10:00 A.M.	HOSTESS ORIENTATION TALK—Central Lounge
10:30 A.M.	COMPLIMENTARY DANCE CLASS—Painting Room
11:00 A.M.	LAW LECTURER—Arras Room (Prom. Deck) Subject: Introduction to Law—Basic fundamentals and their effect on every-day living.
11:00 A.M.	GOLF CLINIC—Taormina Swimming Pool Sharpen your shots.
11:00 A.M.	PING-PONG TOURNAMENT
11:00 A.M.	ITALIAN LESSON in the Auditorium (Prom. Deck, fwd.)
11:30 A.M.	TRAVEL TALK ON CURACAO and hints on custom regulations given by our Cruise Director. What to see, what to do, what to buy —Arras Room.
11:30 A.M.	TRAP SHOOTING—Weather permitting (Foyer Deck, aft.)
12:30 P.M.	LUNCH—Capri and Tivoli Restaurants
FROM 12:00 (noon) to 1:30 P.M.	BUFFET AT THE SWIMMING POOLS—Weather permitting (Lido and Boat Decks)
2:30 P.M.	MOVIES in the Auditorium (Prom. Deck fwd.)
2:45 P.M.	BRIDGE LECTURE FOLLOWED BY DUPLICATE BRIDGE—Promenade Deck, portside
3:00 P.M.	UNATTACHED PARTY—Arras Room (Prom. Deck) Come and drink the "bubbly". Single swing with the DE MICHELIS, Orchestra.
3:00 P.M.	INFORMAL CARD PLAYERS GET-TOGETHER See RENATA in the Card Room (Promenade Deck)
3:30 P.M.	PASSWORD—Arras Room—with EVELYN
4:15 P.M.	FASHION SHOW—Arras Room—Organized by E. M. I.
4:30 P.M.	TEA CONCERT—Central Lounge (Prom. Deck)
4:30 P.M.	TEA DANSANT—Arras Room (Prom. Deck)
5:00 P.M.	SNOWBALL JACK-POT BINGO—Arras Room
5:00 P.M.	MOVIES REPEATED—Auditorium (Prom. Deck fwd.)
6:30 P.M.	CAPTAIN'S COCKTAIL PARTY for 1st sitting passengers—Painting Room (Prom. Deck)
7:00 P.M.	LATEST NEWS AND WEATHER REPORT ON TV (Enclosed Promenades, Central Lounge and Painting Room)
7:00 P.M.	GET-TOGETHER GALA DINNER—1st sitting
8:15 P.M.	CAPTAIN'S COCKTAIL PARTY for 2nd sitting passengers—Painting Room (Prom. Deck aft.)
8:30 P.M.	MOVIES REPEATED—Auditorium (Prom. Deck fwd.)
8:30 P.M.	DANCE MUSIC, FUN AND GAMES—Arras Room with the DE MICHELIS Quintet for 1st sitting passengers
8:45 P.M.	GET-TOGETHER GALA DINNER—2nd sitting
9:00 P.M.	INTERNATIONAL STAR-STUDDED FLOOR SHOW—for 1st sitting passengers—Arras Room
9:45 P.M.	HORSE RACES—Painting Room (Prom. Deck)
10:15 P.M.	DANCE MUSIC, FUN AND GAMES—Arras Room with the DE MICHELIS Quintet for 2nd sitting passengers
10:30 P.M.	INTERNATIONAL STAR-STUDDED FLOOR SHOW—for 2nd sitting passengers—Arras Room
10:30 P.M.	LATE MOVIES repeated in the Auditorium
FROM 10:30 P.M. to 00:30 A.M.	OPENING OF "PORTOFINO TAVERN"—Dance to the "NEAPOLITANS"—Boat Deck aft.
FROM 10:30 P.M. to 1:00 A.M.	DANCING in the Painting Room (Prom. Deck) Music by the "FORTI" Orchestra
11:00 P.M.	OPENING OF THE ATLANTIC NIGHT CLUB—Dance to the "I LIGURI" Orchestra (Foyer Deck aft.)
00:30 A.M.	GALA BUFFET—Central Lounge (Prom. Deck)
FROM 00:30 A.M. to 2:30 A.M.	MUSIC INTERLUDES—Portofino Tavern—
2:00 A.M.	SNACKS and PIZZA PIE—Atlantic Night Club (Foyer Deck aft.)

SHIPBOARD DRESS:
The Suggested Dress For This Evening Is FORMAL

RELIGIOUS SERVICES: 9:00 A.M. and 5:30 P.M.
HOLY MASSES—in Chapel (Foyer Deck)

SAFE DEPOSIT BOXES FOR VALUABLES
Are obtained free of charge at the Information Desks (Foyer Deck)

VISIT OF THE BRIDGE
permitted from 9 to 11 A.M. and from 3 to 5 P.M. while at sea.

PHYSIOTHERAPY—A qualified physiotherapist is available each day from 8 A.M. to noon and from 3 to 7 P.M. on Lido Deck, Gymnasium, Tel. 326.

BIRTHDAYS · ANNIVERSARIES—All passengers who have birthdays, anniversaries or wish to arrange private parties are requested to notify the Maitre d'Hotel at their earliest convenience.

GIFT SHOP—Anything from a needle to an anchor . . . you will find in our boutique located on the Leonardo and Gioconda Foyers. Stop in and see the wonderful Italian craftsmanship.

PASSENGERS' TALENT SHOW—That show is coming your way. If you can sing, dance, play a musical instrument or tell stories, please register with our Hostesses now!

All passengers belonging to Rotary, Lions, Kiwanis, etc. are invited to register their names at the Pursers' offices.

NOTE: HOURS SHOWN ARE SUBJECT TO CHANGE

Above: Gazing at the endless horizon, *Michelangelo* powers across the ocean on the 'Sunny Southern Route'. (Richard Volpe)

Left: Like all transatlantic carriers of that era, planned entertainment activities were rudimentary by today's cruise ship standards. This is a daily programme for *Leonardo da Vinci*. (Alberto Imparato collection)

The 'Sunny Southern Route' generally provided ample opportunity to enjoy the lido and swimming pools. Traditional deck quoits were supplemented by skeet shooting from the stern – a popular participation and spectator sport. (Author's collection)

It was one of the greatest spectacles of an ocean passage, a neatly choreographed Italian Line performance set on a seemingly infinite stage. Midway between Genoa and New York, *Michelangelo* and *Raffaello* converged on the vast expanse of the Atlantic Ocean. Passengers flocked to the open decks, where the salt-laced wind, accelerated by the ships' 26-knot momentum, tore at clothing, slip streamed hair and raged in the ears of the eager spectators. Each onrushing vessel cleaved the waters, the flared bow casting waves aside disdainfully. Suddenly the two huge ships were parallel, almost impossibly close and separated by a boiling, turbulent concoction of turquoise and foam. Whistles saluted, ensigns dipped and flares lit the blue, blue sky. (Giancarlo Criscuolo collection)

Above: As the crowds lining the decks cheered and waved, there was a momentary connection, then within an instant voices and faces faded on the breeze, leaving only the lacy wake. The drama of these encounters serve as a fitting analogy of the ships' careers – eager anticipation, followed by an all too brief moment of glory and then a tragically drawn-out demise. Both rendezvous and careers might have been fleetingly transient, but the memory is imprinted on the mind of all those fortunate enough to have experience it. (Author's collection)

Below: One of the delights of passage on a passenger liner of the era; seemingly endless days cocooned with a good book, gazing out at the sea from the enclosed promenade. This is on board *Raffaello*. (CRDA, Italia – Alberto Imparato collection)

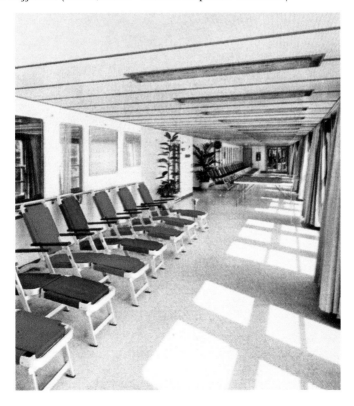

Each class had their own children's room with toys, and it appears any excuse was used to stage a party with the requisite jelly and ice cream and other sweet fare. Older children were also catered for, as John Mattessich recalls:

> One of my fondest memories of the two great ships was the arcade room. There were about five pinball games in the arcade, and it was, naturally, a great place to meet kids of my own age. On one of the pinball machines, an older boy turned several screws, which removed the back panel and exposed the credit wheel. This allowed anyone to manually set the number of credits. Typically, a player received a credit by inserting the required amount of money or by getting a high score. With the back cover removed, however, it was possible to adjust the credits to a large number, allowing one to play the entire day for free! Vandalism, yes. Yet I suspect the crew knew about this little secret, and decided not to do anything to end our fun.

Without exception, young travellers seem to have enjoyed crossing on Italian ships far more than any other nationality. The crew genuinely cared for the welfare of little ones, rather than regarding them as an unwelcome irritant, which was frequently the experience on board North European rivals. (Giancarlo Criscuolo collection)

Evenings were invariably a leisurely but formal experience, with class divisions rigorously enforced. Cocktails in an adjacent bar were a prelude to dinner, proving then as now to be a voyage highlight. Generally there were no informal options (with the exception of room service) and therefore the majority of meals were taken in the dining rooms at assigned tables. This could prove a blessing or a curse, as Richard Volpe recalls when crossing Eastbound on *Raffaello*:

> As we requested, we had the second seating in the Ritz Restaurant on the foyer deck. We were seated with four other people, all single. Amy and I were the only married couple. The six of us got along

famously and dining with them was always an eagerly anticipated event. The food and service were excellent. Our table steward always made sure we had something we truly enjoyed even if it was something not offered on the menu. Unfortunately, our table mates disembarked at Algeciras and were replaced by two couples that were traveling together. They were from Germany and spoke only German and very little Italian. I spoke English and even less Italian than they did. Amy spoke only English. The fact that they were friends coupled with the language barrier all but completely excluded us from any conversation. The entire complexion of our dining experience had changed.

Traditional Italian recipes prevailed, although there were plenty of options for any Americans unwilling to experiment.

Long before television talent shows, chefs on board the Italian flagships were transforming exquisite food into works of art. The artistic experience went beyond the kitchens, however. Achille Lanata, who served as a waiter on board all three ships, recalls how staff were specially trained to extravagantly cut mundane apples, oranges and bananas into floral shapes at the table in front of passengers. Arguably the most elaborate offerings were the late night buffets, with their rich aromas and colourful displays. In First Class especially only the best was expected; cliché's prevailed, with caviar liberally dispensed, and the pasta was flawless.

Dancing to a resident band, listening to recitals, adjourning to a favourite bar or maybe a film in the cinema were popular post-dinner activities. Traditional shipboard games including 'horse racing' nights were also organised. They may not have had sky diving or dodgems, but in 1970, long before Royal Caribbean claimed to have installed the first ice rink at sea, *Raffaello*'s theatre was adapted for an American couple to provide skating performances. Furthermore, some of the most interesting distractions these liners could offer are unavailable on any of their modern counterparts. Bridge and engine room visits were a regular feature, as Richard Volpe recalls: 'Amy saw how much I loved all aspects of the ship so she arranged for me to take a tour of the engine room. I remember, at one point of the tour, looking up and seeing the starboard propeller shaft eye level and a little above me. It was only then that I realized how far down in the hull I was standing.'

Preparing some of the finest Italian cuisine afloat is *Raffaello*'s First Class kitchen. (Alberto Imparato collection)

Above: Dinner was always a highpoint of days at sea, as seen in the Capri restaurant on board *Leonardo da Vinci*. (Author's collection)

Below: *Michelangelo*'s First Class ballroom provided a perfect venue for evenings spent dancing across the Atlantic. (Author's collection)

Of course despite appearances, it was not always plain sailing. Fellow passengers could be irritating and cantankerous. Parasitic ship bores or the needy and lonely might latch onto the unsuspecting, who remained a captive audience with no means of escape. In an era where sharing a cabin in Tourist Class was common practice, roommates' sleeping and bathroom habits could create a tense atmosphere.

For many, seasickness, which John Maxtone-Graham describes as 'that diabolical combination of pitch and roll [that] set some demon to work in the inner ear', was the scourge of an ocean passage. Remedies were as numerous as they were invariably ineffective. Brandy often featured in some form, as it had in 1842 when Charles Dickens, writing arguably the finest description of a sea voyage ever penned, so eloquently described the sense of surreal, miserable ennui the condition engendered. Despite the Italian ships' bulk and stabilisers, when the going got rough, those afflicted invariably took to their cabins, to lie it out as Dickens recalls 'with no desire to get up or get better, or take the air, with no curiosity, or care, or regret, of any sort or degree' – a state he so aptly summarises as 'not ill, but going to be'. As well as physically debilitating, sufferers might also have to endure the ribbing of those fortunate souls who appeared immune to motion.

Fortunately, whether it was providing a remedy for seasickness or dealing with more serious conditions, all three ships were equipped with state-of-the-art medical equipment in the hospital, including X-ray machines and full operating facilities.

Sometimes even storms could foster friendships. Richard Volpe recalls:

On the third day in the Atlantic, we encountered a major storm. The speed of the ship had been reduced to almost a stop for approximately 6 hours as the seas pounded the vessel. Waves were breaking over the bow and as the ship pitched forward, the bow would disappear for what seemed to be an eternity. Ropes were put up throughout the ship in the public areas but most

In the trough; *Michelangelo* encounters another large wave on 12 April 1966. (Claudio Serra collection)

of the passengers stayed in their cabins. I spent a good part of the day walking around the ship which seemed to be deserted. I don't think I saw more than twenty people that entire day. The balance of that time I spent in the Manhattan Lounge on the promenade deck with two bartenders, Franco Capone, another Franco and a waiter named Raimondo. The four of us talked and told stories while they plied me with Stingers from the bar. They claimed that the mixture of crème de menthe and brandy kept you from getting seasick. It must have worked because that evening at dinner, I was one of only a handful of people in the dining room. For the next few months, whenever the *Michelangelo* docked in New York, Franco and Franco would call me and we would get together. Amy and I even had them over the house for dinner.

Fortunately, such conditions were the exception rather than the rule, and the lido lifestyle on the *Rotta del sole* invariably prevailed. The longer voyage time on the Mediterranean route compared to North European rivals was a blessing, allowing passengers to settle into a languid routine.

The relaxed atmosphere that endured through the voyage invariably changed on the last night out. With bills to pay, onward travel to arrange or confirm and a sense of apprehension, the tension was tangible. The morning of arrival, especially for novice westbound passengers, generally prompted an early start. Lining the decks, they witnessed the seemingly impossible sweep under the Verrazano Narrows Bridge, the emotional sight of Lady Liberty to port and the emerging mass of Manhattan to starboard. Passage up the Hudson afforded a grandstand view of the famous spires of New York skyscrapers, as well as a muffled prelude to the noise and energy of the city. It was a sensory shock after so many days of the endless horizon and the simplistic, self-contained rhythm of shipboard life. Almost abreast of the towering Empire State building, the ship slowed again as two or maybe three tugs bustled around.

Once the current and wind had been assessed with the assistance of unsecured tugs and their 'toy town' whistles, the ship pirouetted and edged alongside Pier 90. Like all Manhattan super piers, the

Journey's end; *Raffaello* lies at Pier 90 New York. (Finn Tornquist collection)

Italian Line's Pier 90 was essentially a lofty warehouse extension of the New York waterfront. Once ashore passengers were confronted by the time-consuming task of retrieving baggage. In theory large letters and colours denoted the location of luggage by class. In practice it could prove an arduous task and often required the assistance of occasionally mischievous, heavily tipped longshoremen. Jaded passengers then had to endure the infamous attention of overzealous New York customs officers, before finally emerging into daylight, to be confronted by a stream of yellow cabs and the pulsating beat of New York City. As John Maxtone-Graham so succinctly put it in his wonderful book *The Only Way to Cross*, 'There was no more effective purgatory in the world than a North River pier in early September. Americans were resigned to it but vulnerable Europeans experiencing it for the first time were quite stunned.'

Crew – Working On Board

In marked contrast to the international (a euphemism for Filipino and/or Eastern European) crews that keep the modern cruise industry sailing, shipping lines of the 1960s still recruited predominantly, if not exclusively, from compatriots.

This undoubtedly imbued each ship with a distinct and special atmosphere. Furthermore, while each crew member was unique and brought their own personality to their work, it seems certain national stereotypes prevailed. For the Italian Line this manifested itself in a warmth of character, loyalty and the maintenance of that precious balance between detached, efficient service and a caring intimacy.

The old adage that oil and water do not mix was as relevant a metaphor on board the Masters as any other major passenger ship. This was further accentuated by a regional divide, with officers, engineers and managers coming primarily from the regions surrounding Genoa and Trieste, while 'hotel' staff and ratings were mainly recruited from Naples and the Umbrian hinterland. What united them was a dedication and devotion to their respective ships.

The work was hard and tiring and shipboard discipline tight, but there was a palpable sense of pride and camaraderie. In transatlantic service the ships returned home approximately every three weeks. Shore leave in New York was limited but also notoriously fraught in this era, with police corruption and

A dining room
steward at work...
(Author's collection)

...and rest. There was little in the way of organized recreation or facilities, but improvised concerts and performances entertained and bonded the crew together. The mess was the focus of activity, offering camaraderie and hospitality to those off-duty. (Giancarlo Orrù – www. michelangelo-raffaello.com)

rampant crime dominating life in the metropolis. One interesting diversion was the football World Cup, in which liner teams competed, including *France* (France), *Bremen* (West Germany), *Queen Elizabeth* (representing the UK nations) and *Raffaello* (Italy), who played it out for silverware and bragging rights. Achille Lanata recalls these matches were generally held on rudimentary pitches in Brooklyn; however, far from fostering international goodwill, they frequently ended in brawls! As the ships turned more and more to cruising, the balance changed, necessitating extended periods away from Italy, with often three or more months of sailing out of Manhattan to the Caribbean and beyond. In an effort to boost flagging morale, the company arranged family reunions during New York layovers.

Although senior officers enjoyed accommodation adjacent to the bridge, the majority of the crew were accommodated deep within the ship's hulls in four-berth cabins. The cramped conditions actually caused few problems since there were no en-suite facilities. Showering, bathing and changing occurred in communal bathrooms down the corridor.

No commentary of the shipboard working life in the 1960s and '70s would be complete without reference to the unions. Of course, union power reached its zenith in this period and was neither restricted to ships or Italy, but poor industrial relations plagued both decades. Egged on by a militant leadership, employees in an insecure and rapidly changing workplace laudably withdrew their labour to retain their rights, but also, increasingly, as an act of defiance and belligerence. Italian crews were renowned for their warmth of personality and attentive service, and they were as important to the Line's legendary reputation as the ships themselves. Nevertheless, sporadic, petulant walk-outs affected the ships' schedules from the beginning, hardly endearing the ships or crew to the few remaining sea-going devotees.

When the vessels were withdrawn with brutally short notice, crew members were laid off and dispersed. Officers, deck hands and many stewards found employment on cargo vessels or one of the new breed of cruise ships. Others found work in the hotel and catering sectors. Nevertheless, the bonds remained tight and it seems to have been a universal maxim that nothing would ever live up to life on board the Italian Masters.

CHAPTER 8

Powering the Masters

Precision engineering in the Ansaldo workshops sees one of *Leonardo da Vinci*'s low pressure turbines under construction. (Ansaldo, Italia – Alberto Imparato collection)

All three ships incorporated propulsion systems that were of conventional design but innovative and complex in configuration. Each featured two sets of Parsons-type double-reduction-geared turbines, comprising one high and one low pressure unit (known as 'father and son') built under license by Ansaldo. The basic design remained broadly unchanged from the day the eponymous inventor sped his prototype, *Turbinia*, among the assembled fleet marking Queen Victoria's Diamond Jubilee at the Spithead Naval Review of 1897.

Advances in engineering ensured that the turbines installed on *Leonardo da Vinci*, *Michelangelo* and *Raffaello* were among the most efficient examples of their kind. The turbines were driven by superheated steam generated from just four huge Foster-Wheeler water tube boilers. On *Leonardo da Vinci* these created 668 psi of pressure at 842°F, sufficient to produce a mindboggling combined output of 60,000 shp (70,000 maximum). On *Michelangelo* and *Raffaello* the pressure of 782 psi at 914°F produced an even greater 87,000 shp (101,000 maximum). Transferring the resulting power to the propeller shafts was one of the most technically challenging aspects of the ships, and was achieved using double-reduction gearing.

So much for convention. Where these ships differed from their predecessors and almost all contemporaries was the location and configuration of the propulsion machinery, which was housed in two distinct and autonomous engine rooms. Although the norm on naval vessels, only the American Blue Ribband holder *United States* (herself a thinly disguised troop ship) had previously incorporated this feature in a passenger liner hull before *Leonardo da Vinci*.

Furthermore, unlike *United States* and the subsequent *France*, whose four-screw arrangements allowed a symmetrical layout, the Italian engineers had to resolve the dilemma of aligning the fore and aft compartments with just two propeller shafts. Therefore, *Leonardo da Vinci*, and subsequently *Michelangelo* and *Raffaello*, adopted an asymmetric arrangement of boilers and turbines, with the forward engine harnessed to the starboard shaft (88.5 metres long on the twins) and the aft one turning the considerably shorter (56 metres on the twins) port side shaft.

Michelangelo and *Raffaello* were the most powerful twin-screw passenger ships yet built – a title that was subsequently relinquished to Cunard's *Queen Elizabeth 2* in 1969.

Separating the engine rooms was a compartment housing two auxiliary boilers and a desalinisation plant. A company first on *Leonardo da Vinci*, the three evaporator and distillation units were capable of producing 600 tons of fresh water per day. These were enhanced on *Michelangelo* and *Raffaello*. Allowing the ships to be self-reliant for fresh water was particularly beneficial for their cruising activity, when the availability of shore-side facilities wasn't always guaranteed.

Electrical demands were significantly higher than for the *Andrea Doria* and *Cristoforo Colombo* necessitating more powerful auxiliary machinery. Air conditioning, lifts, lighting, galley equipment, stabilisers and deck machinery, in addition to the normal hotel services, all placed a heavy demand on the ships' power generation capability. At sea *Leonardo da Vinci* utilised five 1,100 kW turbo-alternators, supplemented by four 600 kW diesel generators when in port, while *Michelangelo* and *Raffaello* had six 1,600 kW turbo-alternators respectively.

Above left: Keeping it all operational were the dedicated engine room crew. Certainly a breed apart, automation might have removed some of the more extreme elements of the job, but it was nevertheless a challenging, noisy, hot and dirty environment. This is a view of *Leonardo da Vinci*'s aft engine room. (Alberto Imparato collection)

Above right: Monitoring the performance of the great turbines, the engine control room on board *Raffaello*. (Ansaldo, Italia – Alberto Imparato collection)

APPENDIX 1

The Masters – Vital Statistics

Name	Leonardo da Vinci	Michelangelo	Raffaello
Builder/Yard Number	Ansaldo/1550	Ansaldo/1577	CRDA/1864
Gross Registered Tonnage	33,340	45,911	45,933
Net Tonnage	17,227	24,572	24,577
Deadweight Tonnage	5,641	9,192	9,337
Length: Feet/Metres	765.8 / 233.43	904.9 / 275.81	904.6 / 275.71
Breadth: Feet/Metres	92.1 / 28.08	101.8 / 31.03	101.9 / 31.06
Draught: Feet/Metres	31.1 / 9.48	30.4 / 9.26	30.4 / 9.26
Speed Top / Service (Knots)	25.41 / 23	31.59 / 26.5	30.42 / 26.5

Appendix 2

The Masters – The Originals

The Italian Line's policy of naming their principal passenger ships after great historical figures was perpetuated with the final three new-builds. In the immediate post-war era they had focused on the Romans Giulio Cesare (Julius Caesar) and Augustus and the favourite sons of Genoa, Andrea Doria and Cristoforo Colombo. The choice of *Leonardo da Vinci* was inspired and *Michelangelo* and *Raffaello* complemented the decision, providing an appropriate climax for the post-war 'Renaissance Fleet'.

Leonardo da Vinci (1452–1519) Leonardo da Vinci was very much the elder statesman of the three. Born on 15 April 1452, he later moved to Florence, where he worked his apprenticeship. Contemporary accounts portray a tall, handsome, debonair and popular man, blessed with a kind and equitable temperament and an inquisitive mind of startling intellect. The breadth of his skills and knowledge defies belief, with a sublime artistic touch matched by an equally extraordinary scientific and engineering ability. Prolific in his note taking, drawings and philosophical teachings, the one criticism that can be levelled at the great Leonardo is the paucity of his output of finished works. Few survive because few were completed, and he developed an unenviable reputation for unfinished commissions (for which Michelangelo chided him). Nevertheless, finished work provides the world with tangible evidence of his genius; including *The Mona Lisa* and *The Last Supper*. Caught up in political and physical infighting of the autonomous city states of Italy, he ultimately settled in France, at the court of King Francis I, where he died in 1519 at the age of sixty-seven. (Author's collection)

Michelangelo Buonarroti (1475–1564) Physically and temperamentally, Michelangelo Buonarroti was the antitheses of Leonardo. Born 6 March 1475 in the Republic of Florence, the short, hunched figure of Michelangelo devoted himself to an almost obsessive understanding of the human form. This focus soon brought dividends; in 1504, aged twenty-nine, Michelangelo produced his monumental statue *David*, hewn from a damaged slab of marble that had been rejected by other artists. Doubtless a genius and courted by princes and the Papacy, Michelangelo was a cantankerous, irritable and contrary loner. Although wealthy and famous, Michelangelo was renowned for his lack of personal hygiene and austere lifestyle. He rarely washed, slept in his studio and survived on daily rations of water and a crust of bread. Yet for all of his apparent character flaws, referring to himself and 'mad and wicked', the tormented soul of Michelangelo produced many sublime works of art. Sculpture was his preferred medium and the aforementioned *David* together with *Pieta* illustrate his extraordinary ability in this regard. In 1505 he moved to Rome to begin work on the tomb of his patron, Pope Julius II. However, he was soon commissioned by the Papacy for a very different piece; one that, initially at least, he refused. For four years between 1508 and 1512 Michelangelo spent the majority of each day laying horizontal on rudimentary scaffolding, sketching and painting what was arguably his seminal work – the ceiling of the Sistine Chapel at the Vatican. Many artists refer to the sacrifices they make for their art, yet this man's discomfort over such an extended period is impossible to imagine. Blessed with longevity as well as ability, Michelangelo died aged eighty-nine in 1564. (Author's collection)

Raffaello Sanzio (1483–1520) Michelangelo's long life also coincided with the final member of the trio. The youngest of these great artists, Raffaello is generally known in the English speaking world as Raphael. Despite an evident artistic respect, Leonardo and Michelangelo's personal relationship was primarily founded on mutual antipathy. In contrast young Raffaello's almost angelic demeanour endeared him to all. He venerated da Vinci, casting him as Plato in one of his greatest works, the fresco *The School of Athens* in the Vatican's Stanza delle Staegnatura. Leonardo clearly influenced the young Umbrian, but so too did Michelangelo, particularly in the years when the two were the most prominent artists in Rome, between 1508 and 1512. Prolific in output, this mild mannered, hardworking man seemed almost ethereal by nature, living up to his family name of Santi (meaning saint), while also becoming immensely wealthy. Raffaello died on Good Friday, 6 April 1520, exactly thirty-seven years to the day after his birth. (Author's collection)

Bibliography

Books

AA. VV., *TN Leonardo da Vinci* (Genoa, Italy: Ansaldo-Italia, 1960)

AA. VV., *TN Michelangelo* (Genoa, Italy: Ansaldo-Italia, 1965).

AA. VV., *TN Raffaello* (Genoa, Italy: CRDA-Italia, 1960).

Bandini, Simone & Eliseo, Maurizio, *Michelangelo e Raffaello la fine di un'epoca* (Milan, Italy: Ulrico Hoepli Editore S.p.A., 2010).

Braynard, Frank O. and Miller, William H., *Fifty Famous Liners* (Cambridge: Patrick Stephens Limited, 1982).

Braynard, Frank O. and Miller, William H., *Fifty Famous Liners 2* (Cambridge: Patrick Stephens Limited, 1985).

Dawson, Philip, *The Liner: Retrospective and Renaissance* (New York: W. W. Norton & Company, 2006).

Dawson, Philip and Peter, Bruce, *Ship Style: Modernism and Modernity at Sea in the 20th Century* (London: Conway Maritime, 2010).

Dickens, Charles, *American Notes* (London: Penguin Books Ltd, 2000).

Eliseo, Maurizio and Piccione, Paolo, *Transatlantici, The History of the Great Italian Liners on the Atlantic* (Genoa Italy: Tormeno Editore, 2001).

Griffiths, Denis, *Power of the Great Liners. A History of Atlantic Marine Engineering* (Sparkford: Patrick Stephens Limited 1990).

Kohler, Peter C., *The Lido Fleet: Italian Line Passenger Ships and Services* (Alexandria USA: Seadragon Press, 1998).

Maxtone-Graham, John, *The Only Way to Cross* (New York: Collier Books, 1978).

Maxtone-Graham, John, *Liners to the Sun* (New York:, McMillan, 1985).

Miller, William H., *Passenger Liners Italian Style* (London: Carmania Press, 1996).

Miller, William H., *The Last Atlantic Liners* (London: Conway Maritime Press, 1985).

Miller, William H., *Transatlantic Liners* (London: David & Charles, 1981).

Miller, William H., *Great Mediterranean Passenger Ships* (Stroud: The History Press, 2016).

Palmer, Alan, *The Penguin Dictionary of Twentieth Century History 1900–1978* (London: Penguin Books Ltd, 1979).

Scull, Theodore W., *Ocean Liner Odyssey 1958–1969* (London: Carmania Press, 1998)

Walton, Nicholas, *Genoa 'La Superba': The Rise and Fall of a Merchant Pirate Superpower* (London: C. Hurst & Co. (Publishers) Ltd, 2015).

Periodicals

Sea Lines
Shipping Today and Yesterday
Ships Monthly

Websites

www.michelangelo-raffaello.com
www.italianliners.com
www.sshsa.org
www.wrecksite.eu

Acknowledgements

My name might be on the cover, but creating this book has been very much a collective, international effort. I am grateful to all those who have either directly or indirectly brought it to fruition.

First I would like to thank Amberley Publishing for accepting the project and in particular Connor Stait for his patience and guidance.

Special mention and *grazie mille* to Mario Cerbini, Alberto Imparato and Claudio Serra, who generously provided contacts, along with many of the images and anecdotes about the ships. Alberto and Claudio also proof read the draft to identify factual and Italian spelling inaccuracies; any residual errors are entirely my own. Quite simply, this book would not have occurred without them.

I would especially like to thank Achille Lanata and Richard Volpe for their anecdotes of life on board as crew and passenger respectively, thereby bringing the ships to life. Andrew Bryant and John Mattessich's recollections are taken from the 'Project Michelangelo' website with kind permission of Mario Cerbini. For generously allowing me to use images I would like to offer thanks to Giancarlo Criscuolo, Maurizio Eliseo, Uwe Jesperson, Don Leavitt, Hugh Llewellyn, Bill Miller, Ted Scull, Finn Tornquist and Richard Volpe, and, via the 'Project Michelangelo' website, Marc-Antoine Bombail, R. Calcagno, Peter De Monte, Giancarlo Orrù and Francesco Scrimali. Every attempt has been made to seek permission for copyright material included in this book. However, if we have inadvertently used copyright material without permission or acknowledgement, the author and publisher apologise and will make the necessary correction at the first opportunity.

Thanks to Mum, Alex and Becca for your continued encouragement and support. Last and most important of all, I would like to thank my wife Janice, who typed my originally scrawled manuscript, formatted the final version and who has been a trusted sounding board throughout. Thanks so much for helping to make it happen.